MW01228004

TWO ORDINARY WOMEN

TWO ORDINARY **WOMEN**

LIVING LIFE INTENTIONALLY

Patricia L. Headley

Copyright © 2024 by Patricia L. Headley

All rights reserved. Except for brief quotations in critical articles or reviews, no part of this book may be reproduced in any manner without prior written permission from the publisher: Patricia L. Headley, headleypatricia651@gmail.com

Cover design by Susie Rider, Director – Tuyo Print Plus
Cover illustration sourced from Adobe Creative Cloud
Author photo by Ivory House Photography
Book design by Holly Norian

First Edition
ISBN 979-8-9902323-0-3 *(Paperback)*
ISBN 979-8-9902323-1-0 *(eBook)*

"Cupid's Last Rose of Summer" was first published in the August/September 2022 edition of *Mary Jane's Farm* magazine.

For inquiries on live readings or appearances by the author, contact Patricia L. Headley, headleypatricia651@gmail.com

In memory of Ruthanne

CONTENTS

PREFACE

This book is not about illness, death, and dying, though there is some of that too, which can be expected in any story of one's life. Rather, this book is about living a full life despite adversity. It's about two ordinary women, going about their lives, learning to get along in the world, learning to live and play together, learning the myriad challenges of the medical world, and learning how to keep on keeping on. We learned many lessons along the way, but the hardest for me was *there's always tomorrow—until there isn't.*

My late wife, Ruthanne, and I took community education classes; earned higher education degrees; supported multiple theater companies; attended lectures, musicals, museums, art centers, and anything else she found for us to do; all while learning to live together, keeping up with family dynamics, and traveling as much as possible. Then there are all the medical issues we dealt with.

These stories delve into personalities, quirks, accomplishments, disappointments, wonderment, learning, adventure, and a "can do" spirit. Most of the illness issues will come in my next book, with this one sharing the first fifteen or so years of our lives together.

When asked who her audience would be, author Virginia Wolf said, "Ordinary people." I agree with her, and I want this book to be read by ordinary people who might think their own lives too dull to talk about, much less write about.

It's the mundane things of life that make us most human, and frankly most interesting. It's experiences and lessons learned along the way that keep us human. I recently read *The Farmer's Wife* by Kathryn Hamrick. She gave the book to me as a host gift for staying in my house for a week. I think I got the better deal in that exchange. She too, does a beautiful job of taking ordinary everyday stuff and turning it into interesting short stories. I can only hope to match her wit.

Readers who knew Ruthanne will see her personality pop through in nearly every story, and those who know me may find a surprise or two. Ruthanne said more than once, "I'm glad I've lived my life." She truly meant that and wasn't about to let life pass her by for any reason. When I met her, I too, began to appreciate all the things life had to offer. Ruthanne introduced me to hiking and backpacking, something I had wanted to do since I was a teenager. I wanted to backpack in the Adirondacks, and she made that happen. I eventually learned how to plan and lead backpacking trips for others.

Not only did we do planned activities, there was a fair amount of serendipity in our lives and spur-of-the-moment activities. It wasn't uncommon for her to ask, "You want to go see a movie?" at 7:10 p.m., knowing that the movie started at 7:30. I'd give her the list of phone numbers of local movie theaters, and she would call around to see what was being offered, while I somehow managed to change clothes quickly and grab my billfold, and then off we'd go. Once, we walked through the door of the Varsity Theater at 7:29 and the door wasn't yet shut behind us when she said, "We're here, you can start the movie now." The theater owner laughed out loud at that, as if we all thought nothing could happen until we ordinary women arrived on the scene.

Another time we were in Halifax and asked the woman at the front desk of our hotel what kinds of activities were available in the area.

PREFACE

This book is not about illness, death, and dying, though there is some of that too, which can be expected in any story of one's life. Rather, this book is about living a full life despite adversity. It's about two ordinary women, going about their lives, learning to get along in the world, learning to live and play together, learning the myriad challenges of the medical world, and learning how to keep on keeping on. We learned many lessons along the way, but the hardest for me was *there's always tomorrow—until there isn't*.

My late wife, Ruthanne, and I took community education classes; earned higher education degrees; supported multiple theater companies; attended lectures, musicals, museums, art centers, and anything else she found for us to do; all while learning to live together, keeping up with family dynamics, and traveling as much as possible. Then there are all the medical issues we dealt with.

These stories delve into personalities, quirks, accomplishments, disappointments, wonderment, learning, adventure, and a "can do" spirit. Most of the illness issues will come in my next book, with this one sharing the first fifteen or so years of our lives together.

When asked who her audience would be, author Virginia Wolf said, "Ordinary people." I agree with her, and I want this book to be read by ordinary people who might think their own lives too dull to talk about, much less write about.

It's the mundane things of life that make us most human, and frankly most interesting. It's experiences and lessons learned along the way that keep us human. I recently read *The Farmer's Wife* by Kathryn Hamrick. She gave the book to me as a host gift for staying in my house for a week. I think I got the better deal in that exchange. She too, does a beautiful job of taking ordinary everyday stuff and turning it into interesting short stories. I can only hope to match her wit.

Readers who knew Ruthanne will see her personality pop through in nearly every story, and those who know me may find a surprise or two. Ruthanne said more than once, "I'm glad I've lived my life." She truly meant that and wasn't about to let life pass her by for any reason. When I met her, I too, began to appreciate all the things life had to offer. Ruthanne introduced me to hiking and backpacking, something I had wanted to do since I was a teenager. I wanted to backpack in the Adirondacks, and she made that happen. I eventually learned how to plan and lead backpacking trips for others.

Not only did we do planned activities, there was a fair amount of serendipity in our lives and spur-of-the-moment activities. It wasn't uncommon for her to ask, "You want to go see a movie?" at 7:10 p.m., knowing that the movie started at 7:30. I'd give her the list of phone numbers of local movie theaters, and she would call around to see what was being offered, while I somehow managed to change clothes quickly and grab my billfold, and then off we'd go. Once, we walked through the door of the Varsity Theater at 7:29 and the door wasn't yet shut behind us when she said, "We're here, you can start the movie now." The theater owner laughed out loud at that, as if we all thought nothing could happen until we ordinary women arrived on the scene.

Another time we were in Halifax and asked the woman at the front desk of our hotel what kinds of activities were available in the area.

She mentioned something that would take us about an hour or two north of there. "Okay, then. We'll go up there tomorrow," Ruthanne announced. I wasn't startled at all. I never knew what to expect and never knew what was coming next. That was simply everyday life with Ruthanne.

The woman all but fainted. With her hand on her heart and her voice considerably higher, she asked, "Without a plan? You aren't going up there without knowing where you'll be staying or making other plans, are you?"

Ruthanne's nonchalant answer was, "Sure, we can manage that."

One fall, we were out in the yard and the neighbor asked where we'd been all summer. "You should have rented the place out; you were here so little." Perhaps he was right. Personally, I thought we should forgo the house entirely, rent an enormous storage unit, and live in a small apartment. Life might have been easier. Ruthanne often said, "Home ownership is overrated." But she needed a place for all her stuff, and she had plenty of it to fill an entire house.

Ruthanne stood at the opened doors of life and might just as well have said to me, "Come, this is the beginning of our journey together, and what a ride it's going to be." This new world had so many opportunities, I sometimes ached for a moment to sit down. Oh, but she wasn't done with me. In addition to travel, she showed me the world of classical music, the arts, theater, a new family, and gazillions of friends. She'd traveled all over the world and was eager to show it all to me. Our grandson Wyatt said, "If I ever get lost, I hope I'm with Nana Ruthanne, because she's been everywhere and knows everyone."

In our thirty years together, we made our lives as full and beautiful as we could. Enjoy reading as you journey through our lives together. I hope these stories encourage you to put on paper or video the adventures of your own lives. It only takes a bit of creativity to turn the stuff of everyday living into memorable stories.

WINGS

I wish

My heart had wings

And could fly

To your side

To embrace you

With love

Patricia L. Headley

LETTERS

I hadn't intended to cry today, but curiosity made me open those old letters we exchanged during our first four years as a couple. Even after we managed to move to the same town at the same time, the letters, cards, emails, and notes continued. My eyes and heart went soft, simply looking at her handwriting on the envelopes. Who would ever have guessed handwriting to be a tearjerker?

At the time the letters were written and received, they were mere correspondence. Now they were precious jewels carelessly stored in a paper sack and tossed to the back of the closet. I noticed that some greeting cards were mailed to my workplace and sometimes they showed up on the kitchen counter. Memories started rushing into my brain—memories of better times, of a budding relationship, of the opportunity to actually live together, and of all the things we managed to do together throughout the thick and thin of life's offerings.

I knew this was going to be a flashback to sweeter times. What I hadn't expected was the roller coaster of emotions I would experience while reading a sack full of memories. Still, I stood there for the longest time reading and reliving the story of our lives. Remembering so many things long forgotten—the romantic that Ruthanne was, or how generous she was with praise, money, and possessions. I let the tears flow, I smiled, I laughed, I ached. But I kept reading—sometimes through copious tears. I took frequent breaks because my heart couldn't take it all in at once.

I spent a whole weekend going through those letters and used excerpts from them to launch several of these stories. Other source materials include old calendars, medical records, emails, notes, letters from friends, and of course, my own memories.

SERENDIPITY

My real life started the day I met Ruthanne Harstad in mid-August 1985. There was no kiss, but I felt like Sleeping Beauty anyway, waking from a thirty-eight-year restless sleep. As a nontraditional female student with kids in high school, I wasn't sure I actually belonged in a college classroom. But here I was watching this bright, witty, competent teacher impart knowledge to all fifty students in that class. I had a whole class period to do a character study on a person I would soon discover was a thirty-three-year-old brand-new teacher, fresh from her first master's degree. She'd been a nontraditional student too. I saw capable hands on well-sculpted arms. She stood at the chalkboard, reached to the far left and wrote with her left hand until she passed her own body, then moved the chalk to her right hand and kept on writing until again reaching her limit to the right. Most students never noticed these details.

What a life we were to have, but it was serendipity that allowed me to meet Ruthanne at all. At the community college (Indian Hills in Ottumwa, Iowa) I was attending, I perused the college catalog for a variety of class choices. It listed class names, a brief description of the class, and the last name of the instructor. I knew none of those teachers, or whether they were male or female. There were half a dozen literature classes listed, but one name stood out. "Harstad," I said out loud.

Then I said the name again. A third time, I said it for the mere pleasure of hearing the sound. "Harstad, that sounds like a good sturdy name."

I let that sink in for a while. "I like that name. I'll take that literature class."

And yes, *sturdy* is the word I actually used. I walked into that class the first day, apparently a minute or so late, and had to take the only seat left in the room. On that first day, Ruthanne wore a marine blue dress, buttoned to the waist, with a woven self-belt and a full skirt; a delicious presentation. She wore sensible shoes, which I found out later were necessary because many dressy shoes don't accommodate orthotics. Her light brown hair was just short of shoulder length, combed into a sort of pageboy—shiny and clean, parted in the middle. Her cute face emanated wholesomeness. And the sight of those hands sent shivers down my spine and continued to do so for the next thirty years. I knew right away that I had chosen the right literature class, even though I chose it in an unorthodox method.

Her wit came through like the sun on a clean window. She exuded confidence, though she later admitted she was as nervous as a lone backpacker facing a poisonous snake with a bad attitude, because it was her first class as a newly hired teacher. We students didn't detect it.

The second time I saw her, she walked into the long narrow classroom, paced off the front half of it, or about twenty-five students, and said to us, "All of you come with me. The rest, stay here. Another teacher will be here shortly."

Along with twenty-four other students—including Linda, another nontraditional student—I followed her into an empty classroom, and she commenced teaching like she'd been doing it for years. The other twenty-five students stayed put. What choice did they have? This was

Ruthanne's third day on the job and already she was petitioning the dean for a smaller class size and decent working conditions.

"Fifty students in a literature class are way too many. Grading papers alone would allow me no time to devote to my other four classes," she told the dean.

I loved that class, and I adored her, though every time we met in the hallways, there was a traffic jam of words crowding my throat, preventing me from saying much. Hundreds of words wanting to get out. Wanting to say something intelligent. Wanting to let her know I was interested. My heart always did backflips and then tried to stand on its own two feet without wobbling. It never bothered her any. She always knew what to say, and for the longest time I let her conversation carry both of us.

Linda and I continued to sit near the front of the classroom after the move. It eventually dawned on me that we were two of the four nontraditional students in the class, serious about our studies, and much appreciated by this serious new teacher. Linda, Ruthanne, and I quickly became friends.

Ruthanne organized get-togethers with her nontraditional students. She scheduled volleyball, racquetball, book discussion groups, and other ways to spend time together. We always enjoyed each other's company.

Ruthanne spent more time grading papers of students who attended class, wrote well, contributed to class discussion, turned homework in on time, and appeared to be serious about learning. She believed the old Chinese proverb that said, *Teachers open the door, but you must walk through it yourself.* I always thought my writing skills were severely lacking because of all the red marks Ruthanne put on my papers. I felt stupid, sure of flunking this class.

"No," Ruthanne said. "The more I mark it up, the more I believe in your potential, and I want you to learn from that. All serious students get that extra attention from me. I believe in giving students as much effort as they give me."

Years later, she encountered a student who had attended maybe three classes all semester. He asked how his grades were doing. "Trust me," she said, "your F is secure."

We all learned right away that this was not to be an easy class. There was a mountain (or two) of reading, papers to be written, and oral reports to be given. But we serious students worked hard, studied hard, and came out with good grades. Eventually, Linda's son Craig took a class from Ruthanne as well. Ruthanne sent him a gift card, and he sent a thank you note, adding, *I don't know if I'm gonna survive next year if I have to take another one of your classes.*

We all felt this way, but Ruthanne accelerated my journey of learning new things. Here was a strong female who was full of life and willing to share all that with me. Despite having just completed her first master's degree, she was already working on an Ed. S, and she would eventually earn another master's—all while working for a living. She also maintained an active social life. She left me feeling like a sloth. How would I ever keep up with this pace?

I wasn't looking down the road to more education. An associate degree was all I aspired to at that time. But she opened the doors to all sorts of possibilities, including a bachelor's and a master's for me as well. I hardly had time to blink, let alone keep up with all our physical and mental activities, attend school, then find employment and maintain a normal life.

My problem was that Ruthanne was always a quick learner. I definitely was not, and I well knew it. She spent ten minutes studying for her next class period and passed with flying colors. I earned A's too, but mine were hard and sometimes painfully earned. I always got there, but my brain was never on the fast track.

"Will you drive me to class so I can study on the way?" she asked one day. The studying was for a Spanish class and the drive was less than ten minutes. *How does she do that?* I wondered.

We sent little notes to each other daily, sometimes two or three times a day, writing not only the date at the top, but the time of day each was written. We connived to see each other in the halls or other parts of the college campus. She later admitted to driving by my house like a teenager in love for the first time.

I reviewed some of those notes, standing in the walk-in closet with letters spread out all over the place and half a sack yet to be read. And there were more letters in a box somewhere.

We met in August, and by late September we began exchanging letters and notes. What I don't remember is how we exchanged those little notes, sometimes written on a strip of paper, sometimes a full-fledged card. There were poems too, and artistic attempts to be cute, mostly on my part. We did meet often in the "Zoo," the student hang-out place—better known at the student life center.

GETTING TO KNOW YOU

I'll meet you in the Zoo later.

NOTE FROM PAT TO RUTHANNE

I had drawn three desks on a piece of paper, and on each desk was a box. The first box was labeled *this week.* The second was labeled *next week,* and the third, *who cares?* Maybe it was my attempt to lighten her mood from her enormous workload.

Once she had reduced that literature class to a reasonable size, she was better able to do the work required, as well as get to know her students. Several of us nontraditional students began to hang out together in the cafeteria and the Zoo. We often invited this new, incredibly bright, incredibly friendly teacher. She was more than happy to join us, being new in town and to the college. Ruthanne and I soon learned that we both liked to play racquetball and volleyball— the only two sports I have ever cared to indulge in. We began to play racquetball together and found a volleyball team to join. We began to take walks together, whether it was in a city park or around the block.

We continued to see each other as much as possible, sometimes a minute and a half between classes, sometimes a half hour for lunch. We looked for other opportunities to be together, sometimes a college

art show or a musical presentation. Wherever either of us was on that campus, we were always looking to see if the other one was anywhere nearby. Like a person with a parched mouth looking for water, I remember looking through, around, and over other people in the hallways, searching for the one face that would increase my heart rate, but still close my throat in fear of saying something mindless. I think we both knew what was happening, but there was no time or space in those early days to discuss it. That is until our trip to Iowa City, which started out innocently enough.

MAKING A CONNECTION

Hey, Christie asked me to go to Iowa City with her Friday. She apparently has some business with the college. Would you like to go?

NOTE FROM RUTHANNE TO PAT

As I finished rereading that note, I jumped back in time to the day we first met and all that followed, but I also reflected on how my life changed from that day in Iowa City, a mere two and a half months after our first meeting.

Christy dropped us off in downtown Iowa City, and we made arrangements to meet up again later in the day. A gentle but steady rain commenced, but fortuitously Ruthanne had brought an umbrella.

"You can share my umbrella," she said casually. She was holding the curved handle, so I left a courteous six inches between our hands and a respectable but equally distant space between our bodies. I barely stood under the umbrella, half of me staying dry and half not, but I didn't care. This was physically the closest we'd been.

As the day went on, her hand moved up and mine moved down until they were touching, and we left them that way, without any verbal acknowledgement that anything was happening. Eventually, our bodies were so close a piece of paper couldn't slide between us, again with no verbal consent or suggestions. It just happened. Though neither of us said anything, I think we both knew something significant was happening. We were making a connection. Later that evening we did have a discussion and decided the relationship was exactly as it appeared to be.

For the next four years, we had a long-distance relationship. She continued to teach. I finished my AA degree in the spring of 1986, then pursued my bachelor's, doing one semester at Northeast Missouri State before transferring to The University of Iowa. It was Ruthanne who suggested that an AA wasn't the end of my college experience.

In the meantime, I was directing summer camp for the Moingona Girl Scouts for another year, having already directed in the summers of 1984 and 1985. This meant attending college recruitment days, receiving and reviewing job applications, interviewing, hiring, and placing each person into a position on the summer staff, then training the whole staff during pre-camp. After all of that came supervising and eventually evaluating staff. For a few months it was like a full-time job.

One day I was standing in Ruthanne's office, and she asked if I could meet her for lunch the next day. I told her I couldn't because I had to interview camp staff for the coming summer season. Why was I doing the interviewing, she wanted to know. "Because I'm the camp director," I said casually. "It's my job."

"You're the director? You mean I know a real live camp director? This is cool. I know a genuine camp director? You're not a counselor or the cook, but the real deal—a camp director? I went to camp when I was a kid and I fell in love with the camp director," she gushed.

"Yes, I'm the director, and kids often develop crushes on all sorts of camp staff. It's a pretty common phenomenon." I was startled yet amused that she was so excited to actually know a real camp director. I admired her enthusiasm. I always considered myself an ordinary person. I was eventually to discover that she had done some incredible things with her life even though she too, considered herself ordinary.

After graduating from The University of Iowa in 1988, I got my first full-time post-graduate job in Peoria, Illinois as a field director for the local Girl Scout office from September through May and a director their camp during the summer. Every other weekend or so, one of us traveled to the other's town for a visit. In between those visits, I looked forward to her phone calls at 11:00 p.m., because in those days, phone calls were cheaper at that hour. But more importantly I looked forward to the sound of her voice on the phone, and perhaps, she looked forward to mine.

By the fall of 1989, four years after our first meeting each other, she was hired at Des Moines Area Community College. I left what was becoming a toxic work environment, and we both moved to Des Moines. But in the meantime, we tried to maintain a relationship. During the times we did have together in the early days, we discussed the difference between the one who has to leave to drive back home, and the one who stays behind.

"It's the one who stays put that suffers the most homesickness," she remarked during one visit when she would be the one driving home.

"It's awful," I agreed. "I've never in my life experienced homesickness before. It's almost like you see death walking down the sidewalk toward you and it has its eyes firmly planted on yours, and the feeling in the pit of your stomach is painful. And for some reason, incredibly real, just like a tummy ache from some physical cause. It's there and only time makes it go away. It's a deep, painful ache. But if asked where exactly the pain resided, I couldn't have said. It's like a big hole opens up and your heart simply falls into it as if meaning to commit suicide."

"Well, that's a good description," she answered.

THE STUPID STAGE

I have so much schoolwork to do. All the camp stuff I've been neglecting has to be done now...I'd sure like for us to spend at least two evenings a week together.

NOTE FROM PAT TO RUTHANNE

For the first year, when we were still in the same city, we endured what we would later term the "stupid stage," where a new couple loses any common sense they ever had, and those around them watch in awe as they witness a new relationship developing. It's when the couple makes googly eyes at each other or stands very close to each other in group situations, all the while thinking no one else is noticing. It's when you try to spend as much time together as possible, despite all the other commitments in your lives. These feelings and behaviors aren't reserved for teenagers. Adults often plunge into the stupid stage too. We can't help ourselves.

We met in August, claimed November 1st as our true anniversary, and had to spend that first Christmas apart. Before she left town to spend the holidays with her family, Ruthanne gave me a blank book and suggested I write to her every day, even though she wouldn't read any of it until after Christmas break. By this time, we were deeply involved. Newly in love and crazy about each other. You know, hanging around the halls at school hoping to catch a glimpse of each other, and maybe have a few words together, sending little notes back and forth, driving by each other's house, and other newly-in-love behaviors.

Ruthanne was "home" for every Christmas from the year of her birth until the last full year her mother was living. How many people can claim that record? When she was a letter carrier, sometimes being "home for Christmas" meant 9:00 p.m. on Christmas eve, but she was there. She made the effort to be there, and her mother appreciated it.

I started writing in the empty book she gave me. Decades ago, I decided I didn't want to write letters just like everyone else. I wanted my letters to be unique. Anyone who's ever received a letter from me since the early '70s will find it does not start out with *Dear so-and-so.* I got creative at greetings, and the Christmas book/journal continued that tradition.

And then there's the silliness. At least two or three badly written poems, two pages of hand-drawn pictures and a few pages of stickers, all sentimental and expressing affection for her. On one page I made potato prints in the shape of the scientific symbol for woman, along with the bottoms of a pair of feet with the word 'love' on one and 'me' on the other. Using stencils, I drew *I miss you* on another page. Clearly, I had too much time on my hands, even though I mentioned having to study for my botany class. There was even a name poem (the kind where each line starts with the next letter of a person's name), also poorly executed.

The journal's narrative surprised me as I reread it. Not all of it is mushy, new relationship, stupid-stage stuff. I opened up my heart and told her what my life had been like the last decade or so. I talked about our future. In one entry I got philosophical.

...I don't know how much either of us can do to assure that we have geographically compatible jobs, but I intend to try...

Indeed, when a job offer came to me from Waterloo, Iowa, not quite four years after we met, I had to think long and hard about taking it. It would have put me two hours closer to her for sure, but I had only been in my current job a bit more than two years, and I simply didn't see the benefit of starting a new one. In the end, I rejected the job, and, as luck would have it, later that summer we were able to move to Des Moines together.

But on that first year at Christmastime, we spent an agonizing thirteen days apart with maybe one phone call to keep us connected. That was the only Christmas we were ever to spend apart until the year she died.

MAKING WAVES

So, you're moving to Ottumwa. Do these people know what they're getting into? Do they realize their droll little lives will never be the same?

LETTER FROM FRIEND NANCY TO RUTHANNE

In early summer of 1985, when she had been hired at Indian Hills Community College but had not yet moved to Ottumwa, Ruthanne got letters from various people, congratulating her on the job. I counted about eight people complimenting her, but a couple of letters stand out.

Nancy was right. Most people didn't know what hit them. Besides dividing a class of fifty students in half during her first week of employment, Ruthanne began bugging the dean about appropriate desks for her left-handed students. Every time she saw the dean, she'd make some remark about it.

"You know, it's uncomfortable for our left-handed students to have to turn halfway around in order to write something." Another time, "Have you put left-handed desks into your budget yet?" Or, "I still don't see any left-handed desks for our students."

This went on for about two terms. Late in the third term, she walked into her classroom and prepared to teach. Several students came in and remarked about these new awkward desks. Ruthanne looked up and noticed that every desk in the room was for left-handed students. She laughed out loud with that gunshot laugh of hers.

"We will make do for this class, and you right-handed students will get a lesson on accommodating other people's needs. At the end of the class, I would like everyone in these three rows to take your desk with you to your next class and bring one of those desks back here."

She was always practical and easily found solutions to nearly every problem that dared to present itself to her. It always left me in awe.

The second letter I made note of concerning her new job came from Ruthanne's father, Ken. Again, I recognized the handwriting on the envelope.

Indian Hills is lucky to have you on board. I think about the fine qualities you bring. He included a little hand-drawn pie chart, urging her to use it to list the possibilities for her life. The chart included sections called Responsibilities, Risks, Rewards, and Friends. If she ever used the concept, I didn't know about it. But his drawing stayed in the envelope with the letter for all these years.

FOUND MONEY

You really should let me do my own laundry. I'm sorry
I can't seem to remember to empty my pockets.

LETTER FROM PAT TO RUTHANNE AFTER
SPENDING A WEEKEND TOGETHER

I've had this bad habit for years of not checking my pockets before the clothes go into the laundry basket, or the washer. What I left in my pockets that time, I didn't say in my note, but it didn't take her long to come up with a practical application for all the money she found in the washer over the years—ninety percent of it mine.

Almost a year after this incident, she again mentions finding money in the laundry. *I have an idea,* she wrote. *Let's save all our pennies, nickels, and dimes and put them into our vacation fund. We can call it Found Money.*

It could technically be called "found" money, but she knew where it came from and to whom it belonged.

Okay, I replied, thinking that any vacation we took would have to be supplemented with real cash, like a whole lot of twenties or a healthy credit card.

It took two decades of living together for Ruthanne to admit that she continued to keep all my money she found in the laundry. "I've collected a lot of money off you over the years."

"What do you do with it?"

"I put it into the Found Money stash."

Found money wasn't the only source of income she deemed valuable for a vacation savings plan. She had lots of ways of saving for future vacations. "We can also add all the money we get from turning in cans and bottles."

Recycling was not only a hobby for her but a passion. Anytime we took a walk she picked up cans, smashed or not. She did her homework and discovered that in Iowa each county is required to have at least one place to redeem smashed pop cans. Most counties don't make that one place easy to find.

Sometimes she took a plastic grocery bag with her on walks to collect these cans, always netting a half dozen or more. If we happened to take a walk without a bag, she wasn't deterred. Many times, I saw her pick up a smashed can, smack it on the curb a couple of times to extract any liquid still hanging out, and stick the thing in her back pocket. I indulged this hobby but refused to participate in it. Ants also like to crawl around in things like that, and any liquid residue gets sticky. Too much yuck factor.

This hobby took over our garage and almost took over her life. She set up a system to sort out cans by brand name, count them, and put them into bags or small boxes.

"Why do you do all that work?" I asked. "Why not put them all into a big garbage bag and be done with it?"

"Because soda companies will not take a competitor's brand, and the recycling facility wants them to be in bundles of one hundred, by brand."

"That seems silly. Don't they all end up in the same place anyway? I can't believe each company actually recycles their own stuff."

"It's a rule. That's all I know."

"So, they're all afraid of recycling even one can from a competitor?"

"It is what it is," she said.

I went with her once, and only once, to do this chore. Even though the cans were separated by brand name and were counted into bundles of exactly one hundred, some poor schmuck at the recycling facility still had to handle and count each of those cans. We couldn't be trusted, apparently. It took forever as we stood on the loading dock watching him count, while the sun slowly moved from east to west. *If I ever have to do this chore,* I thought, *I'm not going to all that trouble if they are going to do it again anyway.*

After all the cans were counted and accounted for, the staff person wrote it all down, had Ruthanne sign it, then sent it to the office. Off we went to sit in that office waiting room for eighteen eternities while they processed it and wrote out a check. Why cash wasn't good enough, I don't know, but I thought the whole process egregious. *Let someone else do it,* I thought. She claimed she was helping both the environment and the Found Money fund.

She also collected all sorts of plastic bags and other debris, took it home and put it in the recycling bin while stating emphatically, "Humans don't deserve this earth." I would hear that phrase many times during our lives together.

Ruthanne got really creative when it came to her "found money." We owned AFLAC stock and many times over the years they offered stock splits. For a while it was growing by leaps and bounds. She saw this as free income. *Found* income. When an upcoming vacation got near, we'd cash out ten or twenty shares and add that to the stash. We could pretend with the best of them that these habits fully funded our trips.

I never purposely left money in my pockets, even for the sake of the "found money fund," or to feed her fantasy that it was a super fund,

but it also did not change my habits. I'm still not housebroken.

Just yesterday, I found fifteen dollars in the washer. These days, any money I find goes directly back into my own pocket. It does not go into some jar. You could say I launder money frequently. Literally. A couple of weeks ago I was trying to dig out coins from the tiny space in the washer between the spinning part of the tub and the part that doesn't spin. I retrieved three quarters, two dimes, and two pennies. Three pennies are still in there and may have to remain for perpetuity.

Did all that found money ever fully pay for a vacation of more than a weekend? I doubt it, but it gave her something to do besides dealing with health issues and grading mile-high stacks of papers. It gave her something else to get creative with, something else to think about, and something else to feel good about. Who was I to say otherwise?

PLASTIC STRAWS AND OTHER VILLAINS

I'm looking forward to our trip to the Ozarks during Christmas break. We'll stay in Cedar Rapids for a few days then head south.

LETTER FROM RUTHANNE TO PAT

One of the first arguments we had was in 1987, the first time we were able to take a trip together, over a plastic straw. We had spent a few days with Ruthanne's parents, being sure our stay included Christmas Eve, and then left for the Ozarks to hike. We stopped for a restroom break and the ubiquitous snack accompanying such stops. We bought soft drinks, and while filling our cups, Ruthanne insisted we not use the plastic lids. "Those things put too much plastic in the landfill, and they never decompose."

Ruthanne was always ahead of her time, but this was the first of many attempts to teach me how to save the environment. She took the *reduce, reuse, recycle* mantra seriously. She added *repurpose* to that list long before it was popular as well. She once bought me a t-shirt with all those words on it. I wore it until it was almost a rag, then actually ripped it up and put it in the rag bag to be repurposed as dusting rags.

I picked up two straws that day, dutifully leaving the plastic lid behind, but when we got back into the car, she again had a directive. "We won't use those plastic straws either. They contribute to the overuse of landfills."

"I am traveling in a moving car with a full cup of liquid, and I need a straw. This cup is flimsy and I'm not going to take a chance of spilling it all over me," I replied grumpily.

"I was just thinking that we might try to cut down our use of plastic. The cup will decompose, but the straw will take hundreds of years to break down." It was another ten years before I realized that the cup is only partially recyclable, and another ten years before I broke the news to her.

She was forever bringing cups home to toss in the compost bin. She also tossed in empty popcorn buckets from the movie theater. So many things from our house ended up in that compost, a good share of which I did not put there. But perhaps that's why I had the richest soil in the neighborhood.

She truly believed she was helping to cut down on landfill waste. And she was, for the most part, but what she didn't realize was that all those paper cups and buckets have a microscopically thin layer of plastic on the outside. It helps keep food and liquids from leaking out before the contents are consumed. Every time I turned the compost or dug some out to put on the garden, I pulled out dozens of little pieces of plastic. I was baffled for the longest time as to where they were coming from, until one day I was turning the compost and saw one of those cups, only partially decomposed, with its thin layer of plastic barely hanging on.

When I mentioned it to her, she was as surprised as I was. "I didn't know that," she said. "Sorry, I thought I was doing a good thing."

"It's okay," I said. "They're just little bits of plastic, which I gather into a small pile and put in the trash. Most of it does decompose."

Her first lesson as to my stubbornness came on the day of the straw. I stopped talking for the next couple of hours. Many times, over the course of our relationship she expressed frustration that rather than argue a point, I refused to talk about it. I did eventually learn how to stand my ground if I thought I was right. But on this day, it must have sent a powerful lesson, because eventually she apologized. "I'm sorry about the straw thing. You're right, one little plastic straw won't make that much difference."

When we traveled, we used only one of the two or three wastebaskets in a hotel room. This was more from experience than environmental concern. She'd been a motel maid for two weeks when she was a young woman and remembered the job well.

"It's a lot of work cleaning these rooms. We can help by reducing their workload." And that was always followed by a generous tip. One thing motel cleaning personnel never saw in the trash cans we did use were used toilet paper rolls and the paper the new one was wrapped in.

If we were the ones to change to a new roll, she put the paper items in her suitcase to take home for the recycling bin. It didn't matter if we were in Iowa or Ireland, she was forever bringing things home to recycle.

"Do you recycle these?" she would ask flight attendants anytime she got a soda can. When the answer was "no" she'd smash it and put it in her luggage to take home and recycle. I was always finding recyclables in her suitcase that had traveled halfway around the world with us.

Anytime we were in a public restroom she managed to get by with the single paper towel the dispenser provided, urging me to do the same. My friend Barb recently said to me, "Every time I use a paper towel, I think of Ruthanne."

"So do I," I chuckled. "It doesn't change my habits, but I do think of her."

A while back, I heard the woman in the stall next to me go to the sink, wash her hands, and signal the towel dispenser for the single, stingy, little square it shoots out, and immediately signal it again for another one. *Aha!* I thought, *it does take two. I knew it all along.* I wanted to rush out there and thank the woman for relieving me of years of pent-up guilt over the use of an extra paper towel.

We always composted, sorted paper from other trash, and recycled every scrap of paper that ever entered our house. She reused all paper, sometimes by writing on any little corner of a newspaper page or the back of a receipt. Any piece of paper with writing on only one side got cut into smaller pieces and became a stack of scrap paper near each phone in the house. We could have wallpapered the entire house with all those pieces of paper or made a trail around the circumference of the earth, or to the moon. I wonder how many sheets of paper that would take. I was always finding the tiniest pieces of paper with an important note written on it.

"Do you ever do anything with these little scraps?" I asked, "or do you simply write these things down to run them through your brain one more time?"

"It helps me remember things, and I do use them later," she said defensively.

"Paper is the bane of my life," she said many times. As a college instructor, she dealt with papers every day of her teaching career. Her classes—English, speech, literature, reading, and writing—always resulted in mountains of paper in both her office and our home. She hated it that her life consisted of so much paper, but no matter how hard she tried to make those stacks of paper go away, she couldn't reduce it.

The college she worked at did not always recycle, and she saw it as her duty to remedy that, at least in her department. Truckloads of paper came home to be put in our own recycling bin. At our house, we had two of the largest recycling bins available and only the smallest trash container. When she saw expired notices on public bulletin boards, down they came, home they came, and into the bin they went. I understood what she was trying to do, but also recognized she was only one person, trying to make up for thousands of people lacking her environmental philosophy. She never managed to conquer the enormity of it all, but she spent years trying to make a difference.

Straws, on the other hand, she could control. During our entire relationship we never used straws when dining in a restaurant. That I could live with, and in most cases, I still adhere to that little bit for the environment. These days you can buy your own glass or metal reusable straws, which are dishwasher safe and come with their own cleaning brushes. Had they been available in our earlier years, you can bet everyone on our gift list would have received a half-dozen.

I learned a great deal from her about how we are polluting our environment and how it will eventually come back to bite us if we don't do something about it. Willful pollution bothered her so much that she repeated that mantra of hers so many times: *Humans don't deserve this earth.*

She truly meant that. It wasn't a statement made in jest, and she deeply felt the harm humans are doing to our environment. I think about her words and actions quite a bit these days, because our waterways and landfills are full of waste that will never decompose. And of course, she was right all along with her original statement. Because I've come to learn that one little plastic straw actually will make a difference.

LOCATION, LOCATION

I sure enjoyed being with you this weekend. It was like rain after a drought. It was a good weekend, but I think we ate too much.

LETTER FROM PAT TO RUTHANNE

Depending on who was in what location, we were usually two to four hours away from each other by car. We had our weekends though, and that sustained us until we could move to the same city at the same time. In most of my letters, I talked about how it was good to be together, how much I had missed her, and how much I was looking forward to our next time together.

During the week we talked on the phone (not cell phones). It was always nice to hear her voice, but it was all I could do to stifle a bunch of yawns during these 11:00 p.m. calls. My normal bedtime was usually an hour earlier. I wondered how we ended up being in such vastly different locations and how long that situation would last. *Please,* I begged the universe, *let us find jobs a whole lot closer to each other.* The universe eventually answered.

TEACHING, LEARNING, AND MOVING ON

I'm going to have to take a bunch of papers with us on the trip so I can get them graded.

LETTER FROM RUTHANNE TO PAT

I can't recall how many times Ruthanne said this or how many times she continued to do this the whole time she was teaching. She always had stacks of grading to do. Often those papers traveled with us wherever we went, whether the destination was domestic or international. Sometimes they got graded and sometimes they just enjoyed the journey. Such was the life of a teacher of English, literature, reading, writing, and speech. My work was done at the end of the day. Hers was a constant companion.

"Your papers are better traveled than most of you are," she told her students.

Despite all the work that accompanied her wherever we went, we did find time to socialize. She held a *Color Purple* party and afterwards I said in a note, *Have you noticed that several of us from your first literature class are now pretty good friends? Most of those who sat up front anyway. It was the atmosphere in your class and your friendly manner that helped bring us all together.*

In a note to me one day she said, *I am becoming more and more resentful by the minute of being required to be on campus and in my office so many hours. We have to check in with the secretary when we arrive on and leave campus.*

And then, a few weeks later, another note came. *I'm so tired of this place. Smokers in the bathroom, irresponsible students, bizarre and sexist administration, no days off between quarters, payroll screw ups, and on and on.*

It was so unusual to have a normal-sized class that she actually commented on it the one time she had a small one. "I have only eighteen students in communications class. The name quiz should be easy, as should the end-of-term grading."

The name quiz always happened on the first day of her classes, for every class she taught. She had the students stand in a circle with her. They tossed a tennis ball to each other while stating that person's name. By the end of that first class, she knew every student's name, despite the class size. Very few of her students could say the same.

She watched as several colleagues left for places with more reasonable working conditions, smaller classes, and professional treatment for instructors. After Ruthanne finally moved on to another job, one of her former colleagues wrote her a letter in which she mentioned, *I'm cutting back on my adjunct classes. I had too many overload ones.*

During that first term, she wrote me a note saying she had a tough meeting to attend. She knew there would be a confrontation and she wasn't sure of the outcome.

I responded by writing, *Enjoy your meeting tonight. Don't ever feel humiliated. Feel proud that you are taking a positive step.* Neither note went into detail about the issue at hand, and these many years later, I don't remember. Those days were tough for her.

Within a year of meeting, we began to think that someday we

might be able to live together. In one note she mentioned, *we both need to work on getting jobs in the same place at the same time.*

By the fall of 1986, Ruthanne was still in Ottumwa teaching overload classes. I graduated from community college, did my summer as a camp director, and moved on to Northeast Missouri State University (NMSU). I stayed there one semester and became disillusioned about their Recreation program. It felt like they were teaching me to be a gym teacher. I had no desire to be a teacher of any kind. That semester, I took eleven classes. I learned a lot, but I'm surprised I had time to breathe.

Five of those classes were for a lousy half credit each. Yet we spent as much time in each of those classes as any other. At semester's end, there was a physical test, a written test, and sometimes an oral test for each class. I had to know and successfully demonstrate all fourteen steps to the tennis serve, and so on.

Through all that, Ruthanne and I managed to see each other several times, and of course, the letters continued. When I began complaining about the trajectory I was on, Ruthanne suggested I apply to The University of Iowa, her alma mater. I would never have thought of transferring if she hadn't suggested it, but she always had a solution.

I was accepted into their Leisure Studies program, and in the spring of 1987, I found myself living in Iowa City. At the time I didn't recognize the irony that this was where we first knew we were to be a couple and where we both loved to hang out.

After finally graduating with a degree in Leisure Studies, I found a job in Peoria, Illinois. There went our hopes of living in the same town together, let alone in the same house. After a year, I got my annual evaluation. The biggest complaint my supervisor had was that I was a self-starter, and that I was too competent at what I did. I noticed that she had been spending enormous amounts of time in the office of her supervisor, the executive director. I wondered how either of them ever got anything done. Maybe they didn't have enough to do.

I continued to do my job as efficiently as I could, and my constituents were happy with my work. But I couldn't have said I was happy working in that office environment. I started wondering how I could move on. I loved the people in the field, and the summers at camp, directing a staff of thirty for the benefit of 130 girl campers, was splendid. But the office atmosphere was stifling and the condescension from my immediate supervisor was more than I cared to take long-term. Eventually, I became careless, and we had a showdown.

My supervisor and the executive director asked me to meet them in the staff house at camp. I was told to sit on the couch in the living room. It was an old, beaten-down couch with barely any support in the cushions. I sat with my knees higher than my waist. They brought two chairs from the kitchen table, placed them in front of me, and sat down. I immediately recognized their ploy: Intimidation by being in a higher physical position than the opponent. I almost laughed out loud at their assumption that I hadn't also taken a psychology class or two. But I let these two play their game.

They asked questions. I sat stoically quiet and waited to see how this day was going to end. I think they thought they got the best of me, my life would now be destroyed, and wouldn't I be so sorry I didn't play the scared little employee?

Unfortunately for these two arrogant supervisors, I wasn't intimidated in the least. I'd had enough and was prepared for almost any outcome. They asked me to do something I wasn't willing to do, and they fired me. They did me a favor. Now I could move on with my life and try to fulfill my promise to Ruthanne that someday we would be together in the same city, in the same house, and we could live the life we had wanted for four long years.

Amazingly, within two months, we made that happen.

MOVING TO DES MOINES

I got a new job. I'm going to Des Moines to work at the community college there.

LETTER FROM RUTHANNE TO PAT

About that same time, I wrote a letter complaining about the working atmosphere at my job. *We have to check in and out of the office. Carol is still practicing snooper vision, and Val still thinks I should be spending a good share of my day in her office asking her for advice on how to do my job. Fortunately, Lisa hasn't invited me to lunch anymore so she can pick my brain about what I think of my boss and then tattle on me.*

In a subsequent letter, I explained the snooper vision reference. *Carol has the habit of grabbing some papers, then walking down the main hall until she gets to our shorter hallway, housing four of us field staff. Then, as if the stuff she was reading was so blessed interesting, her legs just somehow forgot to keep on walking, she stopped for long periods of time. She hung out there listening to our conversations until another person came along and interrupted her snooper vision. And that's how I knew we were being snooped on; someone else in the office alerted me to it and I am not saying who.*

The letters continued between Ruthanne and me, and I decided to start looking elsewhere for employment. I was sending out resumes, doing interviews, and hoping for the day we could land in the same city. And then serendipity blessed us both in 1989.

Moving to Des Moines was great news for her and I was happy she got a new job, but it meant increasing the physical distance between us. For a while, I was still stuck in Peoria in a job I was disliking more and more each day. Then I was fired, and Ruthanne was spending the summer working as a forest ranger in the Trinity Alps of northern California.

We packed up her stuff, drove it to Des Moines, and put it in a storage unit. All that summer we exchanged letters, wondering how we could manage to get both of us moved to Des Moines. In the end, I stopped looking for jobs and turned down one I'd been offered in Waterloo, Iowa. Then in early August, at Ruthanne's suggestion, I went to Des Moines and rented an apartment for us. I still had no job but felt sure that this move together to the same city, in the same household, would somehow work out.

I was reading the want ads daily, but we had both moved to Des Moines, and we were elated that we wouldn't be donating so much tire rubber to the roads of Iowa and Illinois.

BALL GAMES

I'm going to have to leave some things at Deb's house for a while. Once we have a place to live, I can come back over and get them.

LETTER FROM PAT TO RUTHANNE
BEFORE THE MOVE TO DES MOINES

I had to make two trips back to Champaign-Urbana in the fall of 1989 to pick up the rest of my belongings, a five-hour interstate drive each way. On one of those trips, I didn't get home until 11:00 p.m. I was so tired, I wanted to go right to bed and forget about the world for a few hours. I had decided to leave all my stuff in the car until the next day. It could wait. Sleep was imminent.

But Ruthanne was full of questions. She was sitting in her recliner, papers all over her lap and around her on the floor. She had settled in, knowing her bedtime wouldn't be for at least two more hours. "You look tired. How did you stay awake during the drive?"

"I listened to a ball game."

"Really?" she asked, astounded.

Listening to a ball game on the radio was not one of my favorite pastimes. I like a couple of sports, but I like being a participant, and even then it needs to be either volleyball or racquetball. Sports wouldn't make it in the top ten of my favorite pastimes, if I were ever motivated to make such a list. I don't read about sports, I don't listen to sports, and I don't discuss sports. It's the first section of the paper I've been throwing into the recycling bin every morning since we moved to Des Moines.

Football never made sense to me. I always argued that they should give each of those boys their own ball to play with, so they don't have to fight over just one. I guess at a minimum they could try giving a ball to each team and see how that played out.

The few times I've been coerced into watching baseball, I nearly died of astoundingly complete, death-defying boredom. Nothing happens out there for hours. To ward off total brain atrophy, I start reading all those ads encircling the playing field, when suddenly someone hits a homerun and the whole place gets excited. People jump out of their seats and start tossing things into the air like God came home. Maybe those spectators are better at staying on task than I am. Their revelry is my only clue that something exciting happened.

Then there's basketball, which has way too many rules, and turns—and twists—and guards dancing around with the enemy and practically embracing them, or maybe creating some sort of new dance. I also don't get all that running back and forth, only to cover the same ground a million times. It's too much for me to comprehend. I do know what it means when the ball drops into the basket.

Is golf really a sport? I don't get the appeal. You stand around doing nothing and wait for one to three other people to take their turns. Then, hallelujah, it's your turn to use this odd-looking stick to send a miniscule ball hundreds of feet away, hoping it will fall into an equally miniscule hole in the ground. A hole so far away they have to stick a flagpole into the ground to give you a hint where to aim. Then the whole group climbs into a cart and drives to the next stop, again using the flagpole as a guide, and this pattern continues all morning. A whole morning is wasted getting a mere three and a half minutes of exercise, assuming the actual physical part of swinging the funny stick takes about twenty seconds. Most people can get that much exercise going to the refrigerator during television commercials. And you don't have to leave the house or purchase weird equipment. In other sports there is a possibility of raising your heart rate a bit. With golf, the heart barely wakes up.

However, at least some of these venues offer pretty good hot dogs, brats, chips, popcorn, candy, and other goodies. That's a plus, and it gives you a reason to leave your seat.

"What game were you listening to?" Ruthanne asked.

"Uhm, well, uh, I guess it was maybe the Dallas Cowboys."

I leaned back on the couch, intending to close my eyes for just a moment. It was already an hour past my bedtime and my concentration was waning. I felt the energy draining from my body and thought I might soon fall into a pile of mush on the couch. But she had yet one more matter on her inquisition list.

"And?"

"And what?" I asked lazily, my eyes still closed.

"Who was the other team?"

In my tired state I scrambled desperately to remember even one moment of what I'd heard on the radio that evening. I admitted to myself that I really didn't know who the first team was, let alone the second. But she seemed to accept my first answer, so I thought I was at the top of my game in making up another team name and confidently said "Well, I, uh um, I think it was the Red Sox."

Laughter spewed up out of Ruthanne's chest like a Yellowstone geyser and continued to bubble like a big ole pot of boiling water waiting for its next pink lobster. Her fun went on so long I began to wonder if I had the skills to recognize the signs of a seizure. One hand wiped away copious tears while the other clutched her chest. Her mouth opened several times, but that full-throated, hearty laughter prevented coherent speech. Her whole upper body shook with such mirth, it finally dawned on me that she was having fun at my expense. But I had no idea what was so funny. Finally, after a full minute or so of such folly, which I think she enjoyed way too much, she was able to sit up straight, take a deep breath, wipe her eyes for the last time, and speak.

"That must have been some game."

JOB HUNTING

The only ads I'm finding for jobs are at fast food places, though there is one for a Kitchen Helper. I don't know if I want to do that again. I did that fresh out of high school.

PHONE CALL FROM PAT TO RUTHANNE

"It would only be temporary, until you find a real job," Ruthanne suggested.

"But they'll say I'm overqualified."

"You will say in your cover letter that you are looking for something professional, but in the meantime maybe you can help them out."

It amazed me how she could always see a solution. I did just that, explaining to a potential employer that I needed a bit of income, and they needed kitchen help, so maybe we could help each other out. During the interview, the head dietician thanked me for my honesty and gave me the job.

For three months, I cooked French fries in the kitchen of Valley West High School. It made me remember those days of working in the kitchen of the Ottumwa Hospital when I was seventeen. I don't recall that we served a lot of fries in 1965, but I learned about working in a commercial kitchen, from how to arrange silverware for customer use, to how to arrange the cash from the cafeteria till at the end of each day. I learned how to set up a food tray with condiments for patients, using thirteen different nutritional requirements.

I liked that early job, and I liked the current one because there were other nice people to work with. I also learned the value of different skills and that someday they might come in handy. I was almost sorry to leave this temporary job. The dietician gave me a nice goodbye and said she was surprised I had stayed that long. "I thought you'd be gone in a couple of weeks," she said.

"Me too," I said. "But it's been nice working here."

I had applied to Youth Emergency Services and Shelter (YESS) as a counselor, but when the director, Susan, read my resume, she offered me a position as Coordinator of Volunteer Programs. Again, they needed a certain skill, and I had that skill. I took the job, and both Ruthanne and I were now gainfully employed. Better yet, we began to settle into our lives together—in the same city, initially in the same apartment, and buying a house within three months. Oddly, we settled in like we'd been doing it for a couple of decades already. And maybe mentally, we had.

NO MEN ALLOWED

The weather report says it's going to be nice this weekend. Do you want to start on the gardens you are anxious to have?

EMAIL FROM RUTHANNE TO PAT

The first spring after Ruthanne and I moved to Des Moines, we were outside doing yard work when a twelve-year-old neighbor kid happened to stop by. He had come to see his buddy Scott, who lived next door to us. But not finding Scott at home, the kid decided to lean on the fence and engage us in conversation.

"Hi," the kid said.

"Hello," Ruthanne said. "What's your name?"

"Matt," he said. "So, what are you guys doing?"

"We're creating a flower bed," I answered.

"By yourselves?"

"Yep," we replied simultaneously.

"So, where are your husbands?"

"We don't have any."

"Well, who else lives here?"

"No one, just the two of us," Ruthanne informed him.

"With no men?" he asked, clearly startled at this revelation.

"Yep, you got it." Ruthanne answered.

"Well, who mows your grass?"

"We do."

"Who shovels your walk?"

"We do."

"Who puts the trash cans on the curb?"

"We do."

"Who takes the leaves out of your gutters?"

"We do."

A few weeks later, as I was up on the roof doing just that, our male neighbor directly across the street, told me afterward that he watched in awe from his living room window, holding a phone in case he needed to call 911. I was in my early forties then. I could still climb a ladder, walk on the roof, hang over the edge, and remove leaves and other debris. I was young enough to still have the chutzpah to do it. Ruthanne, five years younger, was more than happy to let me take on that chore.

"You are one tough broad," she said.

Matt continued his line of questioning, until even he was impressed. "Well, I never heard of such a thing. You do all your own stuff without a man around?"

"Yep," we said in unison again, chuckling as he walked away, shaking his head, apparently not yet sure that what he was seeing and hearing was possible.

Many years later, we decided to offer a women's hiking trip through the Shenandoah Valley. There were five of us, four in pretty good shape, and one quite alarmed that we had planned a ten-mile hike for the first day. Elaine was terrified of that prospect. "That's way too long. Aren't there any shorter hikes around here?"

"That's a four or five-hour leisurely walk, including a few rest breaks," I told her. "At a slow two miles per hour, it should take only a bit more than half a day."

It seemed quite doable to me. Ruthanne, who had hiked and backpacked all over the world—including the entire Appalachian trail at age twenty, viewed it as a walk in the park. Particularly since we were only carrying day packs containing water and lunches, and maybe a bit of tissue for when we had to disappear behind a fat tree. And you can bet Ruthanne had a first aid kit in her pack. She might also have been carrying a package of Oreos for the group.

But Elaine was having none of that, so I got the guidebook out and quickly planned a few alternate walks. "Here's one that's less than a mile round trip, and the book says there are a couple of waterfalls on the way."

"Good, let's do that one," Elaine offered.

Off we went, though two of us saw that as a mere stroll.

"I guess we overestimated everyone's abilities," Ruthanne said softly once we were out of earshot of others.

"I guess so," I said. "I'm going to have to spend time tonight revising everything we were going to do this week, even though the rest of the ones we had planned are four miles or less. We did say we would be hiking our way up the valley, didn't we?"

We got to the trailhead and descended several hundred feet until we saw the first waterfall. It wasn't accessible on foot, so we spent five or ten minutes leaning against a fence, admiring it just below our feet. Then we continued on a few hundred feet to the next and most spectacular waterfall, with a nice cool stream. Since we had plenty of time on our hands with such a short hike, we lingered about an hour, wading around in the shallow water near the edge or dangling our feet off a rock.

We soaked our feet lazily in the cool water, as if they had actually done any real walking for the day. It was a fun respite, and we generally had a good time lounging about. "It is kind of nice, just relaxing here for a bit," Ruthanne admitted.

"Yeah," I said. "The water is cool, and the waterfall sounds soothing. The others are enjoying it. And we have plenty of time to waste."

"That's good, because I'm not sure they've yet considered the uphill walk back to the car, especially Elaine. It's not much if we stop at the halfway point again, but someone will complain."

"Well, there's no other way back," I replied. "There's no hurry anyway, so we'll just have to go more slowly than usual."

"Probably," she said. "Apparently some in this group aren't used to this."

Ascend we did. Halfway up, at the first waterfall we'd earlier encountered, we saw half a dozen Amish women near that same fence, enjoying the waterfall below. A glance to the top of the rise told us their husbands were passing the time of day, waiting for their women to finish their short hike. Ruthanne, being the loquacious one, struck up a conversation with the women. After a while one of the women asked what brought us to this very spot along the trail.

"We're spending a week hiking our way north along the Shenandoah Valley, and seeing parts of the Appalachian Trail as well," Ruthanne told them.

Six wide-eyed women sucked in air all at once. Time stood still as they glanced at each other, until one of them found her voice. "Without your men?"

"It's just us women," Ruthanne calmly answered.

Disbelief planted itself all over the women's faces and one brave one asked, for the benefit of the whole group, I'm sure, "Do you feel safe doing that?"

"We're just fine," Ruthanne said and let the conversation end.

That surprised me, but I was proud she let it go at that. I assumed that out of respect for their cultural beliefs, Ruthanne thought it best not to lecture them about the self-realizing abilities of today's women. Or maybe she knew she would be wasting her breath.

We continued to the top, nodded to their men, who nodded back, and continued on our way. We did, however, get a chuckle out of the women's unabashed shock at our enormous capabilities, and our unabashed, super-sized audacity, sans our men.

ALICE WALKER AND
THE COLOR PURPLE

When we meet tonight, let's visit for a little while, but then we both need to work, work, work. But we can still have some fun. Maybe we can each eat about thirty pounds of chocolate.

NOTE FROM PAT TO RUTHANNE

During that first semester taking Ruthanne's class, when Linda and I wondered if we would make it through, Ruthanne presented an enormous syllabus. There was so much reading we thought our eyes would cross. We were both avid readers, but not used to discussing literature in front of a whole classroom or having to write about what we were reading. Both of us had seen a couple of decades go by since high school.

Linda's husband Tim offered to write one of the assignments for her, but she refused, saying that this was something she needed to learn how to do on her own. I had no such offers, but I did have to give a lot of thought on how to approach some of these writing assignments. One of the many books Ruthanne taught, *The Color Purple,* was different than any I'd ever read. It was my first encounter with an epistolary novel, and it had layers and layers of societal issues to read, discuss, and think about. It was mostly about the subjugation of women, particularly Celie, the main character.

Ruthanne and I both experienced these sorts of men in our lives, and we could relate to many issues in this novel. I dealt with both physical and emotional abuse as I was growing up, and then again emotionally in my first marriage. Ruthanne's father was one of the nicest men I ever met, but other men found ways to put her down.

"No girl will ever pass a chemistry class I teach," she was told while trying to enroll in a high school class.

Ruthanne and some female friends, finding no girls softball team anywhere, asked if they could play on the boys team. They were denied, even though everyone involved knew Ruthanne was a better player than most of those boys, despite her anatomy.

I met similar restraints. In junior high school, I asked why there was no girls basketball team. "Well, there used to be one," my gym teacher answered, "but a girl got hurt once, so the school dropped it." That was the poorest excuse I'd ever heard for oppressive, outright, outrageous, overt sexism. That paternalistic behavior was the beginning of my quiet but slowly growing independence. But I heard many insults as a woman.

"Why should I hire you? You'll just get pregnant and quit anyway," I was once told in a job interview.

A friend of mine wanted to build a home with her husband and was told by the builder, "No woman will ever design a house I will build." Her retort was, "Then you won't be building our house."

A landlord told me about riding around with his highway patrol friend, who observed a speeding car and said, "I hope it's a woman so I can give her a ticket." I never understood where these attitudes about women came from, nor why this man was so arrogant and sure of himself that he felt comfortable relating the story to a woman.

When I was growing up, the females in the house did absolutely every chore that needed doing. Why? Because we were female. We lacked the appendage that would give us permission to sit around on our backsides and do nothing. When I was about thirteen, I was out in the far part of the back yard when my stepfather called me into the house and ordered me to pour him a cup of coffee. The part that still irks me is that the coffee pot was less than a foot away from him. Why did he do it? Because he could. Because he thought it was funny. Because he always was an asinine jerk. No offense to the nice men of the world. He wasn't one of them.

To be sure, none of these incidents were as devastating as early life depicted for Celie, but they did instill a strong sense of "female strength" in us. As a reader of this novel. I was glad when Celie eventually developed her own sense of self-worth. We also had a connection with Celie through all those things men had the power to keep from us, simply because society still sanctions misogyny.

Later that fall, the movie *The Color Purple* was showing in Des Moines. It was a two-hour drive from the college in Ottumwa, but Ruthanne and I made the drive solely to see the movie. Years later, we traveled to New York specifically to see the musical version. We went partly because we loved Alice Walker's books and short stories, partly because Oprah Winfrey (another of our heroes) sponsored it and played the part of Sophie in the movie.

Sometime later, Ruthanne bought a new copy of the book, sent it to the author asking for an autograph for me, then gave the book to me as a birthday gift. It was an immensely thoughtful gift.

The toned-down version of the *The Color Purple* musical didn't come to Des Moines until after Ruthanne died. She would have seen to it that we attended. Sadly, I wasn't prepared to see it without her. Still, I'd like to thank Alice Walker and her character Celie for being such an important part of our lives together and of our constant fight for equality in a hugely misdirected world.

MISERY LOVES COMPANY

Please get well soon. If I could be there, I would fetch you ginger ale, soda crackers, chicken soup, more blankets, and cold cloths for your forehead.

LETTER FROM RUTHANNE TO PAT

Ruthanne wrote this during the semester I was at Northeast Missouri State University (now renamed Truman State University). Four years later, after we were living in the same house, she found out my mantra during an illness was, *Please go away and let me sleep.*

It's not often that I get the flu, but when I do, I go to the bedroom, shut the door, make it as dark as possible, and curl up in layers of blankets to sleep for however many days it takes. I want all humans to go away and let me sleep the deep sleep of a sick body. About twice each day my bladder reminds me that I should exit my cocoon for at least a few minutes. My absences are so short the sheets are still toasty warm when I return. Once a day, I might wander downstairs and test my stomach's ability to hold food. Other than that, I'm hibernating. I'm enjoying the quiet. I'm enjoying the sleep.

When Ruthanne was ill, on the other hand, she wanted company. If I didn't open the bedroom door several times a day, she'd call me upstairs.

"Are you going to check up on me?" she'd ask plaintively. "Are you going to ask me if I need something to eat, or if I have enough blankets?"

"Sure, I can do that. Wouldn't you rather sleep and not be bothered?"

"No, I want to know that you care, that you are checking to see that I'm still alive up here. You can offer me a bowl of chicken noodle soup once in a while."

"Okay, I can come up and check on you every couple of hours. I would think you wouldn't want to be bothered so you can recuperate better."

"Well, it gets lonely up here."

Lonely? I thought. *How can a person be lonely sleeping fourteen to twenty hours a day, waking briefly for some sustenance, and go right back for another marathon sleep? I think the best way to get well is to make the world go away and to sleep as much as possible. What do I know? Misery loves company, I guess.*

THE FIRST DIAGNOSIS

The work is hard here. I hike at least ten to twelve miles a day in the mountains, but I do like it. I mostly give hiking permits, but sometimes have to tear down a huge fire ring someone built and either try to make it smaller or obliterate it altogether. My eyes are getting worse. It seems to be the worst in the bright sunshine.

LETTER FROM RUTHANNE TO PAT

The summer of 1990 was the second that Ruthanne worked as a ranger for the U.S. Forest Service in northern California. That fall, she made an announcement. "I'm going to call the eye clinic at The University of Iowa tomorrow and make an appointment. I had double vision on the way home from work today. I saw two semis when there was only one actually there."

"How do you know that? Maybe there was one in each lane," I suggested.

"Because one was on top of the other. It was kind of scary, because I couldn't be sure if anything else I was seeing was accurate, and I was pretty sure the one on the bottom was the real one."

"How did you manage to get home?"

"I took a chance that I was in the right-hand lane, slowed down, signaled, and pulled off the highway. Then I waited there until my vision returned to normal."

I agreed she should make the call.

"Your chart says we saw you five years ago in June of 1985," the doctor stated.

"Yes," said Ruthanne. "I had optic neuritis."

"What were your other symptoms?"

"I had severe tingling in my hands, fingers, and wrists. And constant fatigue."

"What did we tell you then about a connection between optic neuritis and multiple sclerosis?"

"You said not to worry about developing multiple sclerosis, because there was no evidence that optic neuritis leads to that."

"Well," the doctor said. "We now know there *is* a strong connection between the two. We know that if you've had optic neuritis just once, the risk of developing multiple sclerosis is about fifty percent. We believe you have demyelinating disease. I suggest you find yourself a good neurologist when you get back home."

Ruthanne did just that, getting her first MRI and diagnosis of multiple sclerosis (MS). There really isn't a definitive test to diagnose MS, although an MRI gives doctors a pretty good guess. She found a neurologist who didn't believe in prescribing a lot of medications. This was fine in the beginning, since it would be three more years before the first drug was approved to treat multiple sclerosis. Now there are more than twenty drugs targeting MS symptoms. There is no cure. The approved drugs reduce the chances of relapse, slow the progression of the disease, and make life more bearable.

We would find out several things about MS in the next few months. If the MRI shows lesions on the brain, it's a good indication that MS is, or will someday, be present. MS is an autoimmune disease, meaning the immune system attacks its own body. In this case, the myelin sheath that surrounds nerve cells. When the optic nerve is attacked, it causes double vision, blurred vision, or blind spots, all of which Ruthanne experienced. She often complained of cleaning her glasses frequently, only to continue seeing the world as if looking through a translucent film.

So now we had a diagnosis of sorts. Her MRI showed lesions. It was eventually determined that Ruthanne had the remitting relapsing kind of MS. Though most of her symptoms weren't severe, they were incredibly inconvenient. Constant fatigue, something almost all MS patients experience, affected her for the rest of her life. She didn't take twenty-minute naps like I did; she slept one or two hours sometimes, and it never helped. The fatigue was there before she slept, and it was there after she woke. The fatigue was accompanied by heat sensitivity when the outdoor temperature was above 72 degrees.

Four years after the MS diagnosis, she had an episode where she couldn't focus her eyes or read anything. Her employer hired a person to read student exams and essays to her so she could grade them. In the meantime, steroids were prescribed in hopes her eyes would recover. This inconvenience disturbed Ruthanne the most. "I don't know what I'll do if my eyesight doesn't return to normal. Reading is important to me, both personally and professionally."

"Hopefully, the medicine will do its job," I said. Eventually, it worked.

By the late '90s, her workload was overwhelming, and she had difficulties managing all the paper in her life. She frequently misplaced important papers and had trouble focusing or multitasking.

"I can't take quality notes during meetings anymore," she said. She couldn't keep up with the current pace, so she petitioned the college to reduce her time to eighty percent, having already done the math. She knew it would reduce her lifetime earnings by more than

$100,000. She knew it meant less going into her social security and other retirement accounts. She knew it meant living more frugally. In addition, her classrooms had to be cool, and she couldn't handle early morning classes. The meeting with college personnel posed a few problems when the facilities manager said the expense of putting room air conditioners in all the classrooms would be too expensive. He was clearly unconcerned about meeting ADA requirements.

As usual, practical, sensible Ruthanne provided the solution. "There's already an air conditioner in room 2-07. Can't we make sure all my classes are in that room?" The facilities manager and her dean both let out a big sigh of relief and agreed that it would be possible to make that happen.

In the meantime, her neurologist had retired. She found another one, but he too, was about to retire. She wasn't sure where she would get medical care for her MS. As luck would have it, I attended a health fair with my students and came home with good news.

"I found a neurologist for you," I announced. "There were some people from the MS Society at the Heath Fair today. Two women at the booth both highly recommended Dr. Hughes."

After meeting with Dr. Hughes, Ruthanne started taking daily injections of Copaxone (glatiramer acetate) at $12,000 a month. Fortunately, insurance paid eighty percent of that, but it still required a lot of out-of-pocket money. Thus began five and a half years of nightly injections. She was advised to do this about the same time every day, which she took seriously, and chose 10:00 p.m. They gave her a chart depicting eight sites on the body for administering these injections, with instructions to rotate the sites. Four of those sites she couldn't reach, so I became nurse on those evenings.

Despite continuing problems, we continued to travel. Eventually, I bought her a two-faced watch so we could easily know when it was 10:00 p.m. our time. She was proud of that watch. Because of it, she almost always got her injection on time, but sometimes we had to get creative. Once, I gave it to her while sitting on an airplane waiting for take-off. Another time I administered it in an airport bathroom stall.

If our hotel room did not have a refrigerator, we had to depend on the kitchen staff to store the medication for us. We kept it in an insulated steel thermos, enclosed in a zipped leather case with her name, room number, and phone number on it. And yet, one evening we waited twenty minutes for the kitchen staff to find it. When she got it, she remarked how cold the leather case was.

"I think it's been in the freezer. I hope it still works," she said.

"That could be why it took them so long to find it," I suggested.

I gave her the shot about forty-five minutes late that night. On hearing the story, her doctor's nurse chuckled and said she didn't have to be quite that serious. "You can have an hour's leeway one direction or the other. Just don't make it too far off the regular schedule."

The MS issues continued for the rest of her life. Eventually, she started taking Aricept, an Alzheimer's medication, in hopes it would help her focus and slow memory loss. I'm not sure how helpful it was, as other issues continued to present themselves.

When we were in New York City during the summer of 2007 with our grandson Adam, we were riding on the top level of a Hop-On, Hop-Off bus, and the temperature was exactly 100 degrees. She was feeling the heat more than ever, as we all were.

"Watch this," she said, and I watched as the fingers on her left hand slowly curled into a fist. "I can't stop it."

"Will they go back?" I asked.

"I don't know. We'll just have to wait and see."

About twenty minutes later, her hand began to slowly uncurl. But we needed to get out of the hot sun and get her something cool to drink. After that, she began to carry those little strips of cloth with coolant in them. You soak them in cold water and wear them around your neck, which was fine as long as you had access to cold water. She also bought one of those little fans sold in airport gift shops, which helped some. From that she graduated to a larger battery-operated fan, and from that to a water bottle with a fan on it that sprayed a cool mist when needed.

The worst part of MS for her was the cognitive decline. She felt that immensely. Her brain used to be so quick at everything she wanted it to do, and when it slowed down she became extremely frustrated. Twenty years after her diagnosis, she decided to take a cognitive test.

"You are testing high average," they told her.

That devastated her, because there was a time when she would have nearly qualified for Mensa. Even in high school, she was known as the bright kid in class.

She learned to live with the MS because she had no choice, but she blamed it every time she found it hard to do a task that would have been a breeze before the diagnosis. She did a lot of negative self-talk when these incidents happened. *I wish I still had a brain. I wish you had known me when my brain still worked.*

Most of us failed to understand, because we had been living with high average or average brains our whole lives. We managed to get along with a brain that was functional, but certainly not superior. We all had to study for tests repeatedly and for more than ten minutes.

We learned to live with her MS, but it became a constant in our lives, no matter what else was going on. It was always present and always a consideration in anything we did.

ARE YOU SAVING SOME OF THAT?

Ruthanne, you need to put some flavor in your food.

A FRIEND TO RUTHANNE

After we moved into the house together, Ruthanne saw laundry as her duty, but cooking became my domain, mostly out of self-preservation. I saw no need to be on a constant bland diet, which most of Ruthanne's cooking was.

She led many backpacking trips and took food to numerous picnics and potlucks. Not too many accolades followed. She could cook when she had to, and we both ate it. But ninety-five percent of the cooking chores fell under my unwritten job description. She liked Annie's macaroni and cheese, and I hated it. Still, I ate it when she decided she could cook.

Her food shopping was as simple as her lunch choices. Just before the series of day hikes in the Shenandoah Valley, Ruthanne went to the grocery store and bought canned tuna, canned chicken, and a box of crackers. Every day, this was our lunch, until one day Elaine sarcastically commented on the food.

"What's for lunch today, Ruthanne? Never mind, I'll bet I know exactly what it is. Crap from a can on a cracker."

I did like the poetic rhythm and the alliteration of her complaint.

Ruthanne's bland diet habit had developed way before the MS affected her taste buds. It was before chemo gave her mouth sores, or the kidney dialysis added a strong and permanent metallic taste to everything she ate. She simply liked bland food. Common black pepper was banned from her menu, and the only way she ate onions was if they were cooked to oblivion. Some days, it made my cooking chores challenging.

Except for sweets. When I made banana bread or brownies, or anything else that started out as a batter, she got excited. She also never fooled me one bit when she crept into the kitchen, snuck up behind me, rested her chin on my shoulder, and sweetly asked me her usual question. "Are you saving some of that for Ruthanne?"

Most people would take that to mean a morsel of batter left on the spoon or the beaters. Maybe there'd be a tiny scraping left in the bowl or the pan. Not so for Ruthanne. Her expectations were much higher.

What I left in the bowl would always have made another muffin or an extra tall loaf of banana bread, or perhaps a thicker pan of brownies. She accepted my gifts like they were the greatest treasures on earth, smiled a big grateful smile, and demurely said, "Thank you, Bootter." She created this nickname early in our relationship and pronounced it as one might say *booker*. Why she added the second *t* I don't know. Maybe she was thinking of all the butter in these recipes.

After I gave her the spoon, the bowl, and the beaters, she went to the living room to sit in her favorite chair, extremely happy in that moment of pure bliss. It wasn't much of a gift in my opinion, but it worked its magic on her, which in turn, worked its magic on me.

BEDTIME RITUALS

Anyone who can't find a book to read in this house just doesn't want to read.

COMMENT FROM RUTHANNE TO PAT

We had books in about every room of the house. There were book shelves in the basement, all three bedrooms, the living room, and the dining room. The bathroom had a plethora of puzzle books and a container of pencils sitting on the windowsill. Accompanying the pencils was a pencil sharpener. The kitchen, naturally, had its share of cookbooks, phone books, and manuals for everything in our house that came with one. Thus, I was surprised one evening at bedtime when she asked about the book I had just closed and laid on the couch.

"Aren't you taking your book upstairs with you?" Ruthanne asked.

"No, that's my downstairs book. I have another one upstairs."

"How can you read two books at the same time?"

"I don't know, I just keep the characters and stories straight. Besides, the downstairs book is often nonfiction and the upstairs one is generally fiction, though I do switch sometimes. I can keep then separate."

My first book, near the couch, was daytime reading, usually more serious or more thoughtful or featuring a plot line that needed more concentration. Another book, three magazines, a couple of newsletters, and a puzzle book or two lived on my nightstand at any given time. My bedtime was always two to three hours earlier than Ruthanne's. I like to read at bedtime, something some experts say you shouldn't do. I don't care. I like to read in bed, and contrary to what they say, it doesn't keep me awake all night. I've never allowed much to interfere with my sleep time.

"Weird," she'd say and shake her head.

"How can you stay up all night reading?" I often threw right back at her.

"Because it's a good book. I can't put it down," she answered, as if it were a perfectly normal thing to stay up until the wee hours of the morning reading, when we all had to get up and go to work the next day.

"Yeah, but you read until two or three some nights," I accused.

"It is what it is."

That often ended the conversation, and we never did come to terms with each other's reading habits, even though we often read the same types of books. My regular bedtime was always important to me; hers was not. Sometimes I'd mention my intentions even as I was walking towards the bedroom.

"Well," I'd say, "I'm going upstairs to spend some time with Bill Bryson."

The first time I did that she was startled. Then, realizing I meant my current book, and by extension, its author, she'd chuckle and say, "Well, I hope you both have a good time."

The advantage of being the first to retire for the night is that I never had to put the house to bed. She always made sure the doors were locked and every last light was turned out—something I never had to do in all our years together. It doesn't seem like much, but I just can't seem to remember to turn all the lights out. The door thing I finally trained myself to do.

When I moved to my new house, I had my son-in-law install number pads on my doors. My daughter, Glori, was visiting one day a couple of weeks later, and as we left the house to run errands, I closed the door and started to walk away.

"Aren't you going to lock it?" she asked.

"I did."

"No, you didn't. See if the door will open."

I did, and it did.

As I stared at it dumbfounded she said, "You have to push the lock button."

"Really? You mean I've been leaving the house unlocked all this time?"

"Apparently," she deadpanned.

I have learned about the doors, both front and back, and the garage door. Now the house is secure when I retire for the night. I'm still working on the lights-off thing. At least a couple times a month I come downstairs in the morning to find a light on somewhere. How hard can it be to put the house to bed at night? Apparently, it's beyond my skill level and something Ruthanne never taught me how to do.

We had another ritual since her MS always made her cold. In the winter I'd sleep on the cooler side of the room, away from the heat register, leaving her the warmer side. In the summer, we reversed that, so I had the air-conditioned side, and she had the warmer side. It worked out for both of us.

One of the neatest bedtime rituals was one we practiced for twenty-five years, or at least for twenty-five winters: the pajama game. Our thermostat was set to go down to 60 degrees at 10:00 p.m. in the winter. That was my bedtime; the house was still warm and toasty and so was I. By the time Ruthanne came to bed, anywhere from

1:00 to 3:00 a.m., the house and every square millimeter of her skin were chilly. I, on the other hand, was cozy and snug in my cocoon of blankets. To make life a little more pleasant for her, I would lay her pajamas out on my side of the bed and sleep on them. By the time she got there, they were as toasty warm as if they had just come out of the dryer. She'd put them on, always murmuring her gratitude. Then I'd snuggle up, grateful for the coolness of her skin against my almost-ready-to-burst-into-flame body.

"You can take that?" she'd ask, always startled.

"Yes, it feels good."

"You are one tough broad," she'd say with a sigh.

BUCAROONS

When you come home from your trip, I will make something special for you.

PHONE CALL FROM RUTHANNE TO PAT

"Now that's a good cookie, right?" Ruthanne inquired.

"Pretty darn good," I answered. "I think I'll have another one."

"Ruthanne always provides, doesn't she?" she asked. She had a habit of referring to herself in the third person.

What made these Bucaroon cookies—actually oatmeal chocolate chip—special was the way Ruthanne babysat them, the way she lovingly created the perfect cookie. She put the ingredients into a bowl in the order and method the recipe instructed, unlike my cooking, which is to throw everything in the bowl at the same time and live with the results. If she cooked at all, it was often something for dessert, and she had perfected the Bucaroons. Once she had the dough thoroughly mixed, she put the cookies on the baking sheet, not too close, not too big, not too small. If I happened to be watching or helping, she'd turn it into a didactic moment.

"Don't grease the pans, because if there is more shortening than there is sugar, you never grease the pan."

I had taken six years of home economics, and I didn't know that. I depended on the recipe to tell me, and apparently thought I didn't need to put that piece of advice into my long-term memory. She did keep the oven at a temperature slightly lower than the recipe suggested.

"They cook slower, and come out softer," she promised. "I don't like crispy cookies."

I'm not sure where she set the oven temperature, but I set it at 325 degrees. It seems to work. She was always in teaching mode, though I didn't always retain the lesson. She made sure the oven rack was exactly in the middle of the oven, then waited for the temperature to get to where she wanted it. I tend to throw things into the oven before the pre-heat cycle is done. With many foods, like roasted vegetables, that's not an issue. With baking cookies, I suspect it is. Ruthanne thought so. Once they were in the oven, she'd set the timer for four minutes.

"That was fast. They can't be done already, can they?" I asked, watching her open the oven door.

"No, it's time to turn them," she answered.

"Why?"

"I want them to cook evenly so they all come out toasty warm, melty, and all of them evenly done."

"I think they need just one more minute," she'd say after the second four minutes.

"How can you tell?"

"They still look moist in the center. I want them to be just under done. After I take them out, I'll let them sit on the pan for one or two minutes before putting them on a cooling rack."

"Why?"

"Because they continue cooking on the pan, and I don't want them to get too done. I don't want crunchy bottoms and they need to be just lightly browned."

I never use cooling racks because things, especially freshly baked cookies, tend to fall through the spaces in them all over the kitchen counter. I always use waxed paper. Maybe I should try the racks just once to see what happens. Those bits that fall through the rack do provide a pre-cookie snack.

All of this "babysitting" required a good kitchen timer. I heard so many dings during cookie baking time I thought I was back in school. Like Ruthanne, I too preferred a cookie that came off the cooling rack soft, gooey, and chewy, with the melted chocolate oozing out during each bite or stretching across a span of space when you broke it in two and pulled the pieces apart. There were no hard-crispy cookies to be found in our house. Waiting long enough for them to cool to the touch was torture. Picking them up a tad too soon, they barely held together. The chocolate chips, which had to be Nestlé's Toll House, all melted, sumptuous and living up to their promise of being richer and creamier. The oatmeal offered some token of healthful eating. The two kinds of sugar did their utmost to fulfill the serious job description of ensuring lifelong addiction.

I've since made those cookies several times, following my own rules, and they weren't quite the same. I recently decided to follow her advice and do things just as she would have. I can't believe I'm really doing all that for a cookie. But the last time I made them, they came out almost perfectly. I don't quite have her touch, or patience probably, but I have served them to other people, and I always get compliments and sometimes requests. I wish Ruthanne were here to taste one of them for herself. I know she'd taste one and say, "Good job, Bootter."

FOUR SQUARES

I'll probably arrive at your house about 5:00 p.m.
LETTER FROM MARTHA TO RUTHANNE

Martha, a missionary with the Lutheran church for many years, was a long-time friend of Ruthanne's family. She and Ruthanne met in Guyana when Ruthanne was sixteen and spending the summer there, also as a missionary. They maintained a close relationship, corresponding regularly throughout the years, and we visited Martha in the Kansas City area a few times.

We had invited Martha to visit us in Des Moines and see our new house. What I hadn't expected was the conversation involving Ruthanne's staunch defense of the environment. Specifically, toilet paper.

"Two squares are plenty," Ruthanne insisted.

"That's not so," said Martha. "It takes much more than that."

"I don't see why anyone needs more than two squares; it's just a little dribble. Two squares do the job nicely."

"But why should I limit myself to that?" asked Martha.

"Because of the putrefaction of our rivers and environmental pollution. We need to reduce the amount of waste we send to our rivers and landfills."

"I understand all that," said Martha, "and I do my share, but if I need four or six squares for comfort and cleanliness I'm not going to skimp. There are other ways to help the environment, and I can skimp elsewhere."

"Well, I think we need to do everything we can," Ruthanne pronounced defiantly.

This conversation, which I stayed out of, went on for a bit longer and got mildly contentious. I don't recall how it ended, but they remained friends for the rest of Ruthanne's life. About a week after Martha's visit, a package came in the mail addressed only to Ruthanne.

"It's from Martha," Ruthanne said. "I wonder what she could be sending, she was just here. Maybe it's a thank you gift or something."

The box measured perhaps six or eight inches square and inside the box was a plastic Folger's coffee container.

"Coffee?" Ruthanne asked in surprise pulling it out of the box. "She didn't drink that much while she was here, and she knows we don't drink it."

She pulled the lid off the coffee container and burst out laughing before I could see what was inside. She pulled out a roll of toilet paper and a short note from Martha.

I hope I didn't use too much of your resources, but just in case, here is a replacement.

I guess Martha had the last word in that conversation. I'm not sure she meant it as a joke, although I'm glad Ruthanne took it that way. I still get a chuckle out of it.

MOWER MANIAC

I'm not using the mower anymore. I sliced through the
cord and of all the luck it was the hundred-foot one.

LETTER FROM PAT TO RUTHANNE

So, feeling guilty, I spent my own money and bought *a new*
100-foot cord. The first time I used it I sliced through it too. We now
have a 95-foot cord. We also have a twenty-two-foot one, because I
sliced the twenty-five-foot one as well. I have to figure out how to get the
lawn mowed. I've used that mower all summer and I still haven't come
to terms with it. If the cord isn't falling out, or getting chopped off, it's
wrapping itself around something, usually my legs.

Because of Ruthanne's devotion to the environment, we bought an
electric mower and outdoor extension cords. With this setup a person
could theoretically mow anything up to 125 feet away from the house,
but the cord was always in the way, no matter what.

I was once tethered in a hot air balloon, which turned out to be a
lot of fun. But being tethered to a lawnmower, which is tethered to the
house, is not fun. But I gave it my best shot. Ruthanne was spending
the summer in the wilderness, and I was left to deal with the grass and
the mower cords.

I don't mind doing my part to save the earth and conserve energy, and I tried my best. But I discovered the hard way that once you run over the cords, you're done mowing for the day. Or the week. Or, in my case, until I got over my snit and trudged up to the hardware store to purchase a new one.

In a second letter to Ruthanne that summer, I discuss the mower and its stupid cord again. *It cost $15 for a new one. I only paid $10 for the first one. The second time, I had them put on a new end, and that too, was more than the cord is worth. Plus, I now have all these chopped up short electric cords hanging in the garage.*

I like to mow. I just didn't like the nonsense this mower presented every time I used it. You can't mow in patterns, but in soldier-straight lines. You can't go around flower beds or trees or yard decorations. At the end of each mowed strip, you have to turn the mower around, pick up the cord, fling it out of the way to the other side of the mower, and commence the next strip. Tossing that cord around for an hour or more doubles the effort put into mowing. I began to resent this mower. It growled at me, and I growled right back. No matter how hard I tried, I always ended up running over that blessed, obnoxious, cord.

"I don't think I can keep taking this newly shortened cord to the hardware store and pay ten bucks to put a new plug on the end of it," I complained. "They made fun of me the last time I took it in."

"The grass has to get mowed," she answered.

"Well, what do you want me to do, get a goat?" I snarled.

When she got home, Ruthanne purchased a new rechargeable electric mower. We plugged it in at an outlet in the garage, unplugged it when it was charged, and mowed like the fun job it should always have been. Now I can be friendly to mowers again, and I can do my part for ecology, all at the same time. Plus, I can make all the round and irregular-shaped flower beds I want.

DOING OUR PART

Good news. Des Moines is getting a new recycling program.

LETTER FROM PAT TO RUTHANNE

The city will be handing out green bins like the one *we use for trash, but this will be for all kinds of recycling. We won't have to sort the recyclables anymore. It all goes into one big bin. Apparently, they are huge. I can't wait to see it. You'll see it when you get back.*

And that reminded me of all the things we (mostly she) did for the environment at that house. Before these big green bins came along, we had little green totes in which everything had to be meticulously sorted for Des Moines Metro Sanitation to pick up. Anything they saw in those little tubs they didn't like they would toss right back on the curb. In addition to those tubs, we started a three-bin compost system that I'm still using today.

We also started a rain collection system for all the vegetable and flower gardens I was establishing since getting that new mower. These days you can buy rain barrels just about anywhere. In those days we had to be creative and find an old container that would work.

First, we found a couple of hard plastic fifty-gallon barrels. Where we got them, I don't remember. The only problem is that they didn't have a cover, so they were open to the environment, squirrels, and children. I found more than one squirrel floating in those barrels and was quite concerned about finding a child in one of them some day. I finally put a thick piece of plywood over the top and held it in place with a cinder block. It wasn't pretty, but it did the job.

We found a company who paints lines on streets and parking lots all over town. The paint they use comes in fifty-gallon hard metal barrels. We got two of them. They had metal lids with a metal ring to hold the lid in place. This was an improvement, but they, too, had issues. To get any water for the garden, we had to reach in and hold the container under water until the watering can was filled.

Finally, I started getting rain barrels from garden catalogs, and eventually from home improvement stores. These were advanced technology. There was a small opening in the top with a screen to let the water in, but keeping everything else out, including debris, squirrels, and small children. And near the bottom of the barrel was a spigot. They also had a spot near the top where you could drill a small hole and insert a short plastic hose, connecting two or more barrels to one downspout. Another clever improvement.

I eventually had nine rain barrels on the back of the house, the garage, and my garden shed. Ruthanne, and several friends asked if I really used all that water. There were a couple of summers when I needed absolutely all of them. More than once, they helped me get through to the next rain. And more than once, we were doing one more thing to save resources and maybe help our planet.

CUPID'S LAST ROSE OF SUMMER

Thanks for the grins, the laughs, the pre-cut grapefruit, the flexibility, the cheerfulness with which you face most things.

CARD FROM RUTHANNE TO PAT

Thanks also for the wonderful eggplant parmesan *we had for supper last night. And it had no bug holes in it. Putting used nylon stockings on the fruit helped keep the bugs out. What a clever idea you had. I appreciate all the produce you raise for us.*

But one day she wasn't so sure of my cleverness in the garden.

"They won't pick that rose. They know you're watching."

"Oh yes, they will. I've left them alone with it. They can't resist."

In my back yard, I grew Sweet Autumn clematis, which crept along the top of the seven-foot-tall chain link fence and cascaded in bunches down both sides, creating several horizontal feet of dense growth. In a bit of remaining space, I grew rambling pink roses. In front of those were several other plants including three hibiscuses that needed to be moved to a better spot. Moving them was that day's arduous chore.

"See you in a couple of hours," I tossed over my shoulder as I left the house.

Often, if I'm quiet, I hear bits and pieces of conversations from people walking the quarter-mile loop track beyond my fence. They push strollers, or they jog, run, or stop to use the exercise equipment placed along the grassy areas. Snatches of conversation not meant for my ears come through, but usually only enough to make me chuckle, shake my head, smile, grunt in despair, or wonder if marriage and/or the world of dating will ever get any easier. I heard joys and sorrows, shopping advice, vacation plans, and "husband" complaints.

Often, I heard multiple snippets of conversation as the walkers completed the loop several times. Maybe I should have hung a sign on the other side of the fence warning that I was eavesdropping. I could have almost become a backyard marriage counselor.

On this particular day, an after-school ballgame was going on in the larger empty area of the field, the center of the loop track. On the grass between the track and my fence sat two young teenagers facing my fence. They had no idea I was there. Their conversation was quiet, but I heard the girl say, "Oh look, there's a rose on that bush."

They got up to inspect. Technically, the rose was on their side of the fence, having grown through the chain link. When I saw the boy reach out, I moved just enough to announce my presence. They stopped short, recoiled, and gasped as if they had seen a ghost, nonchalantly gazed a bit longer, then resumed their places on the grass, again facing the fence. I was surprised to see them to sit in the same spot facing the same direction, rather than move on.

That rose was literally my last one of summer, steadfastly clinging to the bush, and I felt possessive about it. Obstinately, I continued to work in the garden a few minutes more, abandoning the hibiscus, choosing a spot where I was easily seen by these two young would-be lovers. I was planning to pick that rose myself to enjoy indoors.

Then, after some soul-searching thought, I reprimanded myself. *Come on, Pat, this young man wants to impress his sweetie by picking this lovely pink rose and presenting it to her with love in his eyes and heart. Let him have the rose, despite it being your last one. Let him have this heroic moment.*

Difficult as it was, I went back to the house, leaving the shovel stuck in the ground with only one hibiscus dug and sitting in a bucket of water waiting to be transplanted.

"That wasn't a couple of hours," Ruthanne said, "it's barely been a half hour."

I told her about the young lovers and my decision to give them an assist. After she made her prediction, I told her she didn't know about young love and the temptation sitting in front of those two teenagers.

"When I go back out, the rose will be gone, as will the sweethearts," I pronounced.

"I can't imagine they'd do that now, after you let them know you're watching."

"Oh, she wanted that rose and he wanted to give it to her. They'll pick it as soon as they see I'm not out there to protect it. Then they'll leave."

"Well," she said with a chuckle, "It's very nice of you to help young love along."

To my surprise, when I went back to finish my digging chores, the couple was still sitting on the grass, still facing my fence, still sitting right where I'd left them. Slowly twirling in the girl's hand was my last rose of summer, my beautiful pink rose. They seemed quite content.

My heart told me I had made the right decision. They both got what they wanted, and I was proud to have helped. Was I playing Cupid? No, Cupid was already on the job. I merely nudged things along. I looked at the young couple again, whispered "You're welcome," and left them to their courtship. I would have other roses.

BACK FENCE CLASSROOM

*Thank you for all the nice flowers you bring into the
house for us to enjoy. And thanks for all the good things
to eat, even kohlrabi, which I know you don't like. I
know you enjoy gardening, and it's nice to see how you
interact with people walking around the trail.*

CARD FROM RUTHANNE TO PAT

I had plenty of interactions with people on the other side of
the fence.

On the other side of that seven-foot chain link fence was a ten-foot
strip of grass. And next to that, was a track that ran the perimeter of a
huge empty lot owned by the school system. An elementary school sat
in the distance. Over the years I had many encounters with students
and teachers and related most of those encounters to Ruthanne. That
day, I saw about thirty second graders all sitting in a perfectly straight
row on the track looking toward my yard.

"Lots of people raise chickens," I heard one of the two teachers say.

I realized that I, and my chickens, had become an outdoor
classroom lesson. I was flattered and I immediately wanted to be a
more active participant. I waved them over.

While one teacher continued to talk, I ran into the house to get some eggs to show them. I showed them the paper bowl of eggs and explained who was laying the blue eggs, the green eggs, the light pink eggs, and the brown eggs, pointing to each chicken and matching it to the eggs it laid.

"Do you see the white chicken in the smaller pen?" I asked. "Would anyone like to guess why she's in a pen all by herself?"

"Because she's bad," one kid suggested.

"Well, close," I answered. "But it's the others who are bad. The others pecked at her so much she has no feathers on the back of her head. I keep her isolated for her own protection. Otherwise, they would keep at it until she dies from her injuries. When she gets better, I'll let her go back out into the bigger area and see what happens. Hopefully the others will behave themselves."

"What do we say to...excuse me, what's your name?" the teacher asked.

"Pat," I said.

"What do we tell her?"

"Thank you," they chorused.

"Now remember," the teacher said, "you are never to come all the way up to the fence unless Pat is out here to talk to you."

"Here's a classroom lesson for you," I suggested. I passed the paper bowl with the eggs in it over the fence and suggested the teacher bring a couple of store-bought eggs to school the next day and compare the color and size of the yolks to the ones from my chickens. "You'll notice the store-bought ones have pale yellow yolks and these will have plump, bright gold yolks."

Another day there were two boys playing on the other side of the fence. "There are chickens over there," I heard one of them say.

Again, I invited them over for a closer look. Much the same lesson was forthcoming, and I asked them if they'd like some eggs to take home. I ran into the house and brought out a dozen and an extra empty carton. "Now you boys be sure to share these. You will, won't you?" They promised they would.

Another time, a boy about ten came up to the fence at the end of the gardening season. "Why are you turning all those things upside down?"

"To store them for the winter," I answered.

He had a blank look on his face.

"Do you know what these are?" I asked.

"Yeah, they're trash cans," he answered.

"No," I said, "they're actually rain barrels so I can collect rainwater."

He thought about that a second or two. "Why do you collect so much rainwater?"

Sweeping my arm to show my vast flower and vegetable gardens, I said, "So I have lots of water for my garden and I don't have to use city water."

That seemed to satisfy him. I said goodbye and patted myself on the back for having given a good lesson in conservation. However, when I went into the house later and related the story to Ruthanne, she, being the teacher, pointed out that I had neglected the most critical component.

"City water costs money, which is an expensive way to keep the garden healthy. Rainwater is free, and it's better for the garden and the environment since it doesn't have all those chemicals in it."

She was right, as usual. Unlike with the eggs, I'd missed a didactic moment.

On another weekend, several years later, I was working in the garden when three girls about age ten approached the fence to talk to me. One pointed to the ground and asked, "What are those?"

"That's acorn squash," I answered.

"Oh, my aunt loves acorn squash," another girl gushed.

"Would you like to take one home to her?" I passed one over the fence.

"Thank you, ma'am, my aunt will really enjoy this."

Oh boy, I thought, *I'm being ma'amed already at the ripe old age of fifty.*

Which, I guess, was better than what another group of girls, about age seven, gave me a couple of years later.

"Hi, old lady," one of them chirped. The moment I unbent my old lady frame and made eye contact with them they started pointing fingers at each other. "I didn't say that. She did."

"I didn't do it," protested the next one.

I watched this blame game a few seconds, smiled and said, "Good morning."

They giggled as only seven-year-old kids can and continued walking.

The track gets used by lots of adults walking for exercise. One summer about five years after we moved in, a couple stopped to visit for a while. The guy asked, "What do you do with those lids over there?"

I turned to see the metal lids of those fifty-gallon paint barrels leaning against the back of the garage. Around the lids was a ring that could be tightened or loosened once placed on the barrel. After I got my newer barrels, I never used the lids, and explained that to the couple, adding, "Do you want them?"

"We'd take a couple," he said.

"You can have all of them if you want," I said hoping he'd take them all.

"We only have two barrels," he responded.

Getting those heavy barrel lids over a seven-foot fence was much more difficult than the eggs and the acorn squash, but we managed, and off they went carrying their newfound treasure.

ANOTHER MILESTONE

I'm surprised you aren't going to the graduation. It's
your third degree after all.

LETTER FROM RUTHANNE'S MOTHER, ORTHA,
TO RUTHANNE

By the summer of 1992 we had pretty much settled into
the house, our lives, travel, and whatever else came our way. So far,
the MS hadn't caused too much trouble except for the constant fatigue
Ruthanne felt, occasional eye problems, and weird but uncontrollable
clenching of muscles.

I was busy running the volunteer program at work and speaking to
hundreds of people about runaway, homeless, and throwaway youth.
One does get an education working at a youth shelter. Many of those
listeners learned that it isn't always the kid who is the biggest problem.
Some of the stories I heard, and told, were chilling.

By 1993 we were pretty much settled in our routines with work,
play, live theater, church activities, family gatherings, and travel.

I taught a reading and writing course at the community college
that fall. By the second week of the semester, I knew I would not be
doing that again. I prefer teaching in a less formal setting.

When I was directing camps, it was easy because I knew the material so well, and there were no tests to give, grade, and disappoint others with. I taught all sorts of skills my staff would find handy when they had to be in charge of a bunch of girls all day, every day for a week at a time. The only tough part was evaluating my staff at the end of the camping season. Most of them got good reviews from me. But I also had to make recommendations about whether I'd again hire some of those staff. Luckily, I got good remarks from my staff.

I like it that you work with us and not over us, one person wrote in our end-of- summer memory book. Though I did have to fire someone once, and I had to mediate more than one squabble, I managed to get all of us through our summers pretty much intact. At the beginning of each summer camping season, I always had my doubts, wondering how I was going to make it to the end. When the end came, I met it with a deep sadness that it came and went so quickly. As long as I was pursuing one interest at a time I was doing well.

Ruthanne, on the other hand, never pursued just one thing at a time. By the summer of 1992, she was teaching full-time (on a 9-month contract). She also managed to schedule a trip to Arizona for the two of us, took us on several trips to Minnesota to see her grandmother, and took a trip to Aruba. She was also teaching as an adjunct at Simpson College, and she finished her second master's degree, this time in Leisure Studies. Actually, this was her third post-graduate degree, since she'd earned a master's in English and also an Ed. S. in higher education.

"What's an Ed. S. degree?" I asked once.

"It's supposed to be a terminal degree for those who have a masters' and want more education but aren't really interested in a doctorate."

"So, you just went for two master's degrees instead?"

"Yep, a lot fewer hoops to jump through."

I was surprised to find out that this super smart woman had her academic struggles too. "I don't know if I can keep up with this teacher intellectually," she said after one class. "I understand it during the lecture, but I can't repeat it or explain it afterwards."

Wow, I thought as my jaw dropped about twelve inches. *I wonder how I made it through one of his classes.*

In checking our transcripts, I discovered she got an A in that class, and I skimmed through with a B, and probably a low one at that.

Another time, she said, "I think I'm going to flunk this next assignment."

"Why?"

"We have to create a budget for a pretend recreational facility or group. I don't know a thing about budgets."

"Ruthanne," I said. "I deal with budgets every summer. I don't actually create them, but I do have to function within them. We can develop a budget for you."

Ruthanne often entered the house and was already speaking as the door was still closing. A couple of weeks after the budget conversation, she charged into the house saying, "Bootter, we got an A."

"Well, good for us," I said, pleased that I could do something significant for her and that she gave me credit for my part.

And that's the way the rest of our lives together went, with me doing what I thought was enough for my personal growth and the world, and with her doing enough for several people.

STATISTICS

You know, you've talked about getting your master's degree for several years now. Why don't you do something about it? Go over to The University of Iowa or even Drake and see what the requirements are.

CARD FROM RUTHANNE TO PAT

When I was working towards my master's degree, I had to board the slowest boat in town. I was working full time, and with Ruthanne, there was always a full social calendar. Something had to be on the back burner. Most semesters I took two classes. But there was one class I put off until the very end and took all by itself, thinking I could devote all my energy and skills to statistics. I devoted boatloads of energy to it, but any skills I had for this subject lay on the ocean floor. Eventually, it came down to being the only thing standing between me and my degree. After the first test, I believed there was no way to get past this last overwhelming obstacle. The class was required, and I didn't have what it took to pass it. *One lousy class, and I can't do it.*

I have never liked numbers. They might just as well be on a piece of paper on which chickens have inked their feet and then walked all over it. I can't properly balance a checkbook. I follow the rules on the back of the bank statement, but it never works. I don't get it. I don't care if I ever do get it. Give me words any day. They make sense.

This statistics class was just what I expected—a lot of gobbledygook. One day, the teacher brought in a jar of marbles, removed one and tried to teach us the rules of probability, while putting the marble back into the jar if it wasn't the green marble she was wanting. I just blinked my eyes and thought, *well, that makes absolutely no sense.* Astounded, I thought maybe she meant to teach us about improbability instead.

In my non-logical mind, I would assume that if you really wanted the green marble, why would you put each extracted marble back in? Wouldn't it increase your chances of getting a green marble if you eliminated all those you had already removed? Most politicians know that. Reducing the competition increases your probability of winning. Why wasn't it so with green marbles? I couldn't wrap any kind of logic around that.

Each new lesson went just about the same. My mantra was, *my probability of passing this class is becoming smaller each day, no matter what color marble I'm going to find. I have no hopes of ever getting the green one.*

Then came the first test—and the results. I was in clinical depression all the way home. Ruthanne met me at the door and asked how things went, knowing how much I was dreading those test results and knowing how much I disliked that class. The door had just opened, and I started bawling. "I'm never going to get this degree. I don't understand this stuff, and I'm never going to. I hate this class. Why does it have to be so difficult? I might as well give up now."

While she had no solutions, she had lots of comforting words and hugs and reassurances that it would work out somehow. Mercifully, she overlooked the drama—not my typical behavior.

I was beginning to think all those hoops a person has to jump through to enter college were a good idea. I didn't jump through them, though perhaps I should have. I was a nontraditional student and began at community college where the ACT was not required.

After I got my Associate of Arts degree I transferred to Northeast Missouri State University. I was nearing the end of my first semester there when a teacher reminded me that the records indicated I hadn't taken the ACT. She promised me that "we" would take care of that early the next semester. What she didn't know, and I chose not to tell her, was that I had already been accepted by the University of Iowa for the next semester. I wasn't going to take her cursed ACT.

I went to Iowa City, settled in, got good grades, and loved being a student there. But toward the end of my second semester, I got a letter in the mail from the admissions office. *We notice you've not taken any entrance exams,* it said.

I thought I'd managed to skip that evil. But I dutifully kept reading to see when "we" would have to take care of that issue. To see when I had to bite the bullet. To my surprise, the letter went on. *While we understand entrance exams are meant to be a barometer of how well a student will do, we've noticed that you are doing extremely well. We also see that you only have one semester left. After a great deal of discussion, the committee has decided to waive this requirement.*

I don't know what the probability of that outcome was, but I wasn't going to mess around with it. I was at my third academic institution. I had gotten the green marble and managed to leave that institution in good standing.

But Drake University, where I applied for my master's degree, required the GRE. I took it and flunked so badly I decided I didn't need another degree after all. I had apparently forgotten everything I had learned in K-12. Not one lesson came back to me.

But Ruthanne and I dug deeper and discovered that the education department wanted their students to take the Miller Analogies Test instead of the GRE.

She suggested I go to the college bookstore to see if they had practice tests a person could buy. I found they had several. I took them home, ripped the pages out and made multiple copies of each. For a month, I used those copies to practice and practice and practice taking those tests. With more than a bit of hesitancy, I eventually took the real test and got a 98 percent on it.

Does that say something about the way my brain works? It was enough to impress the dean. It was enough to get me over one more hurdle and one step closer to thinking I might make my goal after all.

Having gone through all of that, and having met every other requirement, I thought I was ready to take on statistics. This was the last mountain I'd have to climb. I had a decision to make. Was this going to be the end, or was I going to find a way to at least pull a C out of the class?

Luckily, part of our grade was for projects. These I could do, although I got stuck with three other people who really weren't a good fit. Is group work ever really a good fit? Not in my experience. Usually, one person ends up doing all the work. One group member was a woman who lived about an hour away and begged me to come to her house to study together and do our part of our proposed project. What I found out was that she had even less understanding of statistics than I did. How was that possible? I ended up being the teacher. I knew very little, but I knew more than she did. I hated to leave her stranded, but I didn't have the time, energy, or skills to be a tutor.

The other members of our team were two young male students, fresh out of high school, whose idea of working together was to meet fifteen minutes before class started and hurry through it. As a serious nontraditional student, I needed a bit more prep than that. Even with my minimal skills, I knew when a project was mediocre.

The teacher also wanted us to keep a journal that we turned in every couple of weeks. I could write, and I did. I was absolutely honest about my frustration with the class. I complained about those two young whippersnappers, and about my inability to understand even the most basic concepts of statistics. I told her that the quality of our project hinged on getting the four of us on some sort of basic level of communication and planning. I opened up about all my difficulties, including working with a team.

My test grades did improve somewhat, and I got an A out of that class, but I put a great deal of energy into the journal, something I could completely control. For the projects, I did my best, then talked about the process and my contribution to them in the journal.

At that time, Ruthanne and I both worked at a community college, and she was teaching a night class that semester. "Why don't you go with me?" she suggested. "You can go to one of those quiet rooms at the library and study for three hours."

Why she thought a different study environment would improve my chances, I don't know. But I went. Each week it became three hours of grinding, aching work. I did it so I could increase the probability of improving those test scores. At that point, Ruthanne was the only person who believed I could complete the class. I took her advice seriously and got busy.

For each chapter, I started by reading the first paragraph. Then I read it again. And again. When that failed, I reduced it to the first sentence. I read it. I read it again. And again, until I finally understood what it was saying. Sometimes I had to change a word or two to something that made more sense to me. By the second study session, I brought reinforcements—a dictionary and a thesaurus to help translate what I was reading. Translating a foreign language is what it came down to. When I got to the point where I thought I had an inkling of what it said, I rewrote it using my own words to make it thoroughly understandable, to make it something I could remember for a few weeks.

Those handwritten, transcribed notes eventually became my study guide. It's not often you have to write your own study guide, but this drastic tactic was necessary if I was going to pass this class. It was slow, detestable, agonizing, and grueling work. I hated every minute of it.

Those were quiet rooms, and I could hear nothing of what went on outside. Thankfully, no one outside could hear anything from within. Oceans of frustrated tears flooded my study space, accompanied by more than a few unkind words.

Breaking down an entire chapter sentence by sentence—sometimes word by word—was tedious and mind-boggling. My head ached so much I almost became a drinker. Ibuprofen became my best friend. But I stuck with it, worked harder than I'd ever worked for anything in my life to that point, or since, and somehow got through it. I still don't know how I pulled that off, and my final A didn't give me the pleasure it should have. It should have felt much better than it did. Maybe I was too exhausted by then to care.

I think Ruthanne was prouder of the final grade than I was. She certainly suffered through much of the angst, and to the best of her ability offered lots of encouragement and advice. Sometimes in a group of people we would be talking about college difficulties, and she'd say, "Pat, tell them how you aced your statistics class."

I think she earned that grade as much as I did. I don't think I aced it as much as I slid into home plate by the seat of my pants with seconds to spare. You only have to remove one vertical line from a squared off A to make it an F. It would have been that easy to slide that F right onto my transcript.

CHILL OUT

*I am looking forward to our trip together. Finally, we
will have almost a whole week together. The weather
will be somewhat warmer in Arkansas. I'd rather be
spending Christmas break someplace where we can ski,
but this will be fun anyway.*

LETTER FROM RUTHANNE TO PAT

The hiking trip in the Ozarks took us to Petit Jean State
Park in Conway County, Arkansas, near the Ouachita Mountains.

On the way down there, we stopped for breakfast somewhere in
northern Missouri and found ourselves in an ice-covered parking lot.
We barely made it from the car to the restaurant—and barely stayed
upright.

"I hope this isn't an omen for what we are going to see once we
get there," I said. "We aren't going to be hiking on icy trails, are we?"

"Oh no. The farther south we get the warmer and dryer it will be,"
Ruthanne assured me.

She was right. Once we got there it was warm enough to leave our
winter coats in the car. We found a trail and started walking.

The hike wasn't strenuous, and we needed only day packs with lunch, water, a jacket (just in case), and a snack if we were out longer than expected. And there was always the simple water filter. We put our hiking boots on at the trailhead. The hike was gentle on that warm, but not yet hot, day. We spent the morning going mostly downhill, letting me know that about the time the weather turned hotter, we'd be going back uphill.

After a few hours, we encountered a creek, wide and deep looking. I assumed the hike in that direction was over and we'd turn around and go back to the car. Silly me.

"It looks pretty deep," I ventured.

"It's just a little creek," Ruthanne replied.

Hoping to end this hike, I added, "It's flowing pretty fast too."

"It's a piece of cake." Ruthanne instructed in her teacher's voice, "Take off your boots, socks, and pants."

"Really? We're going to parade around out here in our underwear?"

"There's no one else around."

I reluctantly took my boots, socks, and pants off, assuming that we'd be walking across the creek barefoot. I couldn't believe that was her plan, because even I, with very few outdoor skills, knew better than that. But my hiking partner, my teacher, my experienced hiker, had the whole thing figured out.

"Now put the socks and pants in your pack and put the boots back on. As we enter the water, carry your pack in front of you high enough to keep it dry. Are you ready?"

"Um, I guess." *At least I get to keep my boots on,* I thought.

She led the way. I followed, wishing someone had built a bridge there, or maybe cut down a fat tree and laid it across the creek.

"Holy moly," I screeched. "This water is ice cold! It's coming directly from some snowbank on that mountain we drove up this morning." I complained.

"It's just a bit chilly. You'll live through it."

"This is iceberg water!"

By then the water was up to my knees and I uttered a couple of uncharitable words.

"Just keep moving and you'll get through it," Ruthanne said.

I had memories of the Johnny Cash song "I'm Being Swallowed by a Boa Constrictor" and began to quietly sing a parody of it. *"Oh no it swallowed my toe. Oh me, it swallowed my knee."*

From there, I made up my own words. *"Oh my, it's up to my thigh. Good grief it's up to my briefs."*

*"Oh no it's up to my...*Oh, my stars, this is the coldest water I've ever been in," I yelled loud enough for Ruthanne and anyone else in the 3,471-acre park to hear.

"Stop being such a baby," Ruthanne snapped.

When that cold water graced our waists, I began to give thanks to the water gods for not making this creek any deeper. Baby or not, I was getting nervous. Now I appreciated the lesson on holding our day packs high in front of us rather than wearing them on our backs. I trudged on, still complaining.

We made it to the other side, sat down, took our boots off and placed them in the sun. We too, took a spot in the sun, soaking up its welcome friendly warmth.

"We might as well have lunch while our boots dry out a bit," Ruthanne offered.

"And while we dry out," I suggested. We hadn't brought towels.

We opened our packs and took out a small, flat can of salmon and an orange. We shared both as we sat along the side of the trail in our wet underwear and t-shirts, which had wicked water well above our waists. I shivered but was grateful we weren't in a part of the world where we'd have to be concerned about being chased by wild animals in our skimpy attire. Three minutes after we sat down, a man quietly came up onto the bank, walked past us, said "Hi" and kept on moving.

He politely did not notice our lack of attire. I noticed he was still fully clothed.

"Oops, I didn't know there was anyone that close behind us," Ruthanne said.

"I didn't either, and you said we were alone, but I can tell you one thing. After that tortuous creek crossing, this has to be the best dang meal I've ever had in my whole life."

Her acquiescent chuckle answered first. "Yeah, it is pretty good, isn't it?"

By then, with the sun doing its best to dry us off, I relaxed a bit and started asking about her past hikes.

"Is this the kind of food you ate on the Appalachian Trail?" I asked.

"Oh no. With an eighty-pound pack, I couldn't carry any canned food or much fresh fruit. For breakfast, I usually ate a handful of dried fruit and nuts so I could get on the trail early in the day."

"What about the other two meals?"

"I ate a lot of pasta and dehydrated soups; one-pot meals most of the time. Hikers are constantly hungry from all the calories we burn. I used copious amounts of margarine in everything I cooked. I hate fake butter, but I needed the calories, so I used it. I haven't touched the stuff since then."

"So, you never had sweets?"

"Only when we passed through or near a town and could buy a candy bar or something. And a Pepsi," she said with a grin. "They've changed the trail since then, so it's a bit longer. Now it goes through or very close to more towns than it did in 1977. I remember one time, though. A couple of other female hikers and I hiked about five miles in to town one evening after we had set up camp. We found an all-you-can-eat place. We, and I'm guessing a whole lot of other hikers, ate so many hamburgers that the proprietors later had to put up signs saying *No hikers allowed.*"

"How many did you eat?"

"Oh, I don't know, maybe eight or so."

"Holy moly," I said.

"Like I said, we were always hungry. Plus, there was the walk back."

By then, our boots were semi-dry, so we got fully dressed again and finished our hike. The rest was uneventful, though mostly an incline as I had expected. We cooked our supper in our rented cabin and later were standing on the deck when a bald eagle flew right in front of us, maybe ten feet away. What a treat, and what a cool way to end the day.

COLD SHOWERS

Let's see if Bonnie and Steff want to do something together this summer.

EMAIL FROM RUTHANNE TO PAT

That creek in the Ozarks was mighty cold, but it was nothing compared to the showers at Michigan Womyn's Music Festival. This festival was for, by, and all about being a gay woman in a safe place. It ran every summer from 1976 through 2015 with about 2,000 attendees in the first year, increasing every year after that. It's like any other huge gathering, except there are no men. The year we went, in the late '80s, there were workshops and tents selling products made by women. And of course, a large stage offered music every evening by all-female performers.

Food was served in a large open structure, prepared by those attending the event. There were volunteer charts, and everyone was expected to sign up for a job, whether cooking, peeling potatoes, doing dishes, picking up trash, or dozens of other jobs necessary to organize and hold a large event. The only real structure to our day was our time doing whatever we'd signed up for on the chart. Other than that, we were free to wander around visiting the various booths or taking in the views.

The most laid-back aspect was the event was "clothing optional."

"Prepare yourself to see hundreds of women in various stages of dress," Ruthanne advised long before we got there.

Still, it was a shocker to see hundreds of women in—as she'd said—various stages of dress. Many, like me, walked around fully dressed. We met up with our friends, who also preferred to be fully dressed. Our friend Bonnie was not about to let anyone see her naked or partially dressed. One morning, she was changing clothes in her tent and her partner Steff asked, "Aren't you going to pull the tent flap down for that?"

"No."

"Why not?"

"Because no one can see me in here," said Bonnie.

"How do you figure that?" asked Steff.

"Because of the no-see-um netting."

The lesson she got on just what no-see-um netting is, or isn't, helped her decide to pull down the tent flap for future undressing.

After a couple of days walking around in the hot sun, in this bizarre but totally safe environment, we felt the need for a shower. Off we went in search of the shower house.

"That's it?" I asked, shocked at what I saw.

"I guess so," Ruthanne answered.

Three water pipes stuck up out of the ground, standing about seven feet tall, with showerheads attached to the tops. Standing in three fairly neat rows were dozens of naked women, waiting for a turn, each carrying shampoo, soap, and a towel.

"Well, I guess we'd better get in line," Ruthanne quipped. "It might be a while."

"I guess so," I mumbled.

At some point we knew that we too would have to remove all our clothes. But I always wait until I get to the bathroom to get undressed. What I don't normally do is take a shower in the vast, wide-open countryside, with several dozen other naked women gazing in my direction, patiently waiting for me to finish and move on. I nervously stood in line, gritted my teeth, and remained quiet.

As it turned out, that was the least of it. The moment I turned the water on, all thoughts of other women, naked or not, ceased to be of concern. The whole world disappeared, except for what was happening to my head. That water had some powerful jackhammer pressure behind it, and the moment it hit my head, my scalp shriveled, shrank, screamed, and all but bellowed out with intense pain. Coherent thought or speech was impossible except for the first impulsive "Oh…"

The excruciating headache came exactly one second after the water hit my head. Simple, instinctual, survival mode kicked in, telling me to get this over quickly. That water felt like minus eighty degrees, and the agonizing headache continued through the entire ordeal. I didn't think my scalp would ever relax again.

I held my breath throughout the shortest shower I have ever taken. I walked away with my towel wrapped around me swearing I would never do that again. I shivered even as the warm sun smiled at me.

"How was your shower?" Ruthanne asked in a deadpan voice.

"Like taking a bath in the Arctic Circle," I shouted.

"I didn't mind," she quipped. Of course she didn't; she always liked cool showers.

I shot her a nasty look. "Well, hear this. The next shower I'm taking is going to be in a hotel—on the way home, all alone, indoors, with warm water, and all cozy like. And I may stay there for a while. You got that?"

"Got it," she said throwing a sheepish grin my way.

IT'S A WHAT?

Wait until you see my scheme for how to get us assigned
to the same tent. I'm really looking forward to our hike.
Just getting away and being outdoors once again will
be nice. And spending time with you will be extra nice.
LETTER FROM RUTHANNE TO PAT

Four of us—Ruthanne, Linda, Carla, and I—set out in
Ruthanne's car for Missouri's Potosi District, about a five-hour drive
from Ottumwa. Spring break allowed us a bit of time to get away from
it all; Ruthanne from teaching, and the rest of us from classes and
homework.

At the trailhead we divided up the food and cooking equipment
so we each carried about the same weight. Each person carried their
own clothing, toiletries, and sleeping bags. Ruthanne always carried
the first aid kit. She and I carried the tents and the other two carried
the tarps, one for the ground cloth and the other to put over the tents
to keep any rain out. The two-day hike was fairly easy. The first night
we stopped, Ruthanne announced the tent assignments.

"Everyone whose last name starts with an H will sleep in this tent.
Everyone whose last name starts with a G will sleep in that tent." I had

to admit it was pretty clever, since it got both of us in the same tent.

Throughout the hike, any time we stopped at a body of water, Linda built a cairn for all those people who hiked after us to view. Carla was quiet but contributed to daily chores, fetching and filtering water, cooking, pitching and striking the tents. I did my part as well, though by the middle of day two, I was suffering mild sunstroke and presenting a nice sunburn. Ruthanne did what she could to alleviate my symptoms, apologizing for her lack of foresight. Finding a shady spot to put me in was difficult, it being mid-March, long before the trees sprouted new spring leaves. The only shade to be found was a semi-fat tree. She sat me down there and put cool cloths on my forehead.

"I should have made you all wear hats. I'm sorry. I should have realized that there wouldn't be any leaves on the trees this early. Who knew the sun would be this hot this early in the spring?"

We got through that crisis and the rest of the hike was uneventful, until the last evening. We were in a large area with picnic tables. Carla sat down and pulled from her pack a square plastic container measuring about a foot square and 2 inches deep.

Ruthanne was stunned. "What the heck is that huge thing?"

"It's my makeup kit," Carla answered.

"A what? You carried an enormous makeup kit in the wilderness? I can't believe you'd lug that thing around for two days—in the woods."

"You never know when you might need it." Carla began applying makeup.

"You aren't putting that stuff on for our benefit, are you? If so, you needn't bother," Ruthanne said with disgust. "And believe me, the animals don't care either."

"There are men over there. In case they come over, I want to look nice."

The other three of us pivoted to look, and sure enough there was a small group of men about a football field away. The rest of us hadn't noticed, or if we did, it didn't concern us, and we never assumed for a moment they'd come over for a visit.

"Are you kidding?" asked Ruthanne. "Believe me, any serious hiker in that group isn't going to be impressed by someone who carries an enormous makeup kit around in the wilderness."

Undaunted, Carla continued her regimen. Linda and I were silent but shook our heads and went about our business. And no, the men did not come over to visit us, much to Carla's disappointment.

The next morning, we broke camp and headed for home. Conversation was the usual, but as we neared home, Ruthanne asked so many questions about Linda and her husband Tim and their lives together that the name Tim must have imprinted itself on her brain, or at least on her tongue. When we arrived, Tim was there waiting to pick Linda up. Ruthanne got out of the car and went over to shake hands and said, "Hi, I'm Tim."

Tim chuckled and said, "Funny, that's my name too, I'm glad to meet you."

It was a funny moment for the rest of us, but it embarrassed the heck out of Ruthanne. I have fond memories of the two of us and Tim and Linda becoming good friends and doing things together long after that trip. They eventually moved to California but Ruthanne and Tim, being the two intellectual ones, continued to correspond throughout the rest of Ruthanne's life. I still have some of his letters. I still chuckle about that moment they first met, but more than that, I still laugh out loud when I think of that huge makeup kit in the wilderness.

SINK YOUR TEETH INTO THAT

Gorda asked us to come and you know how well they liked you the last time we were there.

LETTER FROM EMMA TO RUTHANNE

I found many letters from Ruthanne's grandmother, Emma. Ruthanne had taken Emma to Hawaii for her 80th birthday, and a couple years later to western Canada to visit family, particularly a family member called Gorda. In this letter, Emma was asking her granddaughter to once again take her on a trip. Emma wanted to go to Calgary, Alberta again. Ruthanne took her and attended a stampede while there.

Several years later, Emma asked Ruthanne to pick her up from her nursing home in Chatfield, Minnesota and drive her to Minneapolis, where she would catch a Greyhound bus to again visit relatives. Ruthanne asked me to accompany her. How well I remember that trip.

We picked Emma up and as we wheeled her by the nurse's station, we knew her dementia had worsened.

"Good morning, Emma," the staff said.

"Good morning, these are my parents," Emma explained. The nurses didn't seem alarmed, so we played along as well.

We put her in the car and off we went. We ate at a French restaurant, where Emma complained loudly of the sauces on all the food. In the afternoon we stopped at a Dairy Queen for a snack. To avoid any loud complaints, dinner was at a more informal greasy spoon restaurant.

Emma seemed to be doing well, and tracking the conversation as well as one would hope. All was going fine, for a while.

"I feel sick," Emma told us.

"What kind of sick?" asked Ruthanne.

"I feel like I'm going to throw up."

"Quick," Ruthanne said to me, "get one of those plastic grocery bags from under your seat and hand it to Emma."

Ruthanne's habit of keeping all sorts of things under the front seats of her car saved the day. I fumbled around, found one, and passed it to Emma.

"Open the bag real wide and hold it under your chin in case you need it," Ruthanne advised.

We quietly waited as we drove to our next destination.

After a while, the upchucking noises and the enormous, overwhelming odor filling the car alerted us that indeed Emma was sick.

"Look for a garbage can," Ruthanne said. "We need to get that out of the car real soon."

It was dark outside, and they don't put lights or reflectors on garbage cans, but I started looking and after a couple of blocks spotted one. "There," I said, pointing.

Ruthanne stopped the car, walked around to Emma's side, opened the car door, and said, "Let me get rid of that for you."

She took the bag, holding it out in front of her, tying a couple of knots in it as she approached the garbage can.

Later, we got to the hotel, checked in, and went to our room, looking forward to doing nothing for the rest of the evening. We watched a little television, did a little reading, and got ready for bed.

"Emma, you should probably brush your teeth really well tonight, and maybe brush your tongue and the roof of your mouth," Ruthanne advised.

"Why?" asked Emma.

"Well, when you've been sick like that it's a good idea to clean your mouth really well."

Off she went to do as suggested, though I'm not sure she actually understood the necessity. In a few minutes Emma came out of the bathroom and said, "I have a problem. My bottom teeth are missing."

Ruthanne and I both sat mute for a bit. We didn't know that Emma had false teeth, or that a person wouldn't know right away that they were missing. It had been a couple of hours since the trash can incident.

Thus began my dilemma. I knew where the teeth were, and I knew how to get there. But did I disrupt our quiet, peaceful evening? False teeth were expensive. But digging around in city trash cans at that time of night did not appeal to me. Nor, I guessed, did it appeal to Ruthanne.

Right about then, Ruthanne saved the day, or so it seemed. "You'll probably have to make an appointment with your dentist when you get home and order some new ones."

We settled down and started reading, but my conscience wouldn't shut up. It nagged and nagged me to act.

"I know where they are," I said rather sheepishly.

"Really?" Ruthanne asked in a loud whisper.

"Yeah, they're about ten blocks from here."

"How do you know that?" Ruthanne was astounded that I was so sure of myself.

"I remember the route we took back to the hotel."

"No way."

"Yep, I can take you right to them."

For once I knew something Ruthanne did not. Her long-term memory was always superb, but on this night, my short-term memory was equal to the task. I knew exactly how to get back to the garbage can. Retrieving the blessed teeth would be another issue. And I didn't know what we would do with them once we got them.

After thinking about it for a few moments, Ruthanne asked, "What do we tell Emma?"

"Well," I said, "tell her we have errands to run."

"At ten o'clock at night?"

"You got a better idea? They might be gone by morning."

"Oh boy," Ruthanne sighed. "Let's go, then."

We were already in our pajamas, propped up on pillows for the ritual bedtime reading. Emma was just preparing for bed as well. It had been a long day running her around for several errands in Minneapolis and checking to see where the Greyhound station was. We were looking forward to a restful night, taking her to the bus station the next morning, and having the rest of the day to ourselves.

"Emma, we're going to run out and see if we can find a snack."

"Okay," said Emma, not questioning the late hour at all.

We got dressed, went to the car, and I navigated us to the trash can.

"You really remember where it is?" Ruthanne couldn't believe that was possible in a big city like Minneapolis. "I'm impressed."

Little things like that always impressed her, as if she was incapable of managing the littlest things. Fortunately, there weren't many people on the street at that hour. We sat in the car a few moments, trying to buck up our courage. "I suppose since she's my grandmother, I'm going to have to do this," Ruthanne stated flatly.

I chose to stay silent.

"There's a cotton glove under my seat. I keep it there to wear when I put gas in the car because I don't like getting those fumes all over my hand. I guess I can wear it and then get rid of it."

She searched for the glove, put it on, approached the trash can, retrieved the plastic sack, and put it in the trunk.

"That didn't take long," I said.

"Yeah, fortunately there was a lot of trash in there and it was pretty close to the top. Let's look for a gas station. I'm not taking all this to the hotel room. We can pull up to the pump, get some paper towels, wrap the teeth in them, and throw the bag away."

I was always amazed that she had the perfect solution. We found a station and used copious amounts of paper towels, which at that hour no one was paying attention to anyway.

At the hotel, Ruthanne gave the teeth to Emma and said, "Look, we found your teeth."

"You did? How did you do that?"

"Pat knew where to look."

"Thanks, I'll just rinse them off and put them back in."

"You can't do that," screeched Ruthanne.

"Why not?" Emma asked, perplexed.

"They're contaminated. We'll rinse them off, wrap them in some tissue and you can put them in your suitcase. When you get home, you can take them to your dentist to have them properly cleaned. Give them to me. I'll take care of it."

My bet is Emma had those teeth back in her mouth the moment we weren't looking.

The job got done and we settled in for the evening once more. The whole ordeal took less than forty-five minutes. I whispered, "I'm glad I still have my own teeth."

"Me too. Good night."

"Good night. You're a good granddaughter, you know."

"Thanks a bunch," Ruthanne said sarcastically, and turned out the light.

PRIDE

Before we head north for our hike, why don't we go to the gay pride parade in San Francisco.

NOTE FROM RUTHANNE TO PAT

"You're in for a real treat today," said Ruthanne.

"Why?"

"Because you are going to see everything."

Our ultimate goal was to do some backpacking in the Trinity Alps of northern California, but Ruthanne and I decided our penultimate goal should be to watch the Gay Pride Parade in San Francisco, having arrived there the night before. Never having seen a Pride Parade before, I had no expectations. I had no clue what she meant by "everything." Most parades leave me thinking, *well, that was nice.*

Enormous crowds were already wandering, undulating, and populating the sidewalks when we arrived along Market Street about 10:15 or so. Most faced the street, randomly hanging around, moving about as fish in an aquarium. Snatches of conversation were hard to avoid, providing plenty of entertainment. Buzzing, talking, screeching, and shouts of pleasure fueled an already excited, ambitious crowd. Some people moved with purpose. Others ambled like dried leaves floating in a gentle breeze on a long lazy autumn afternoon.

As with any parade downtown in a large city, this one offered a plethora of food for those hungry enough to eat standing up or, more impressively, while walking. Popcorn with its warm buttery smell, greasy pizza slices, tacos dripping with tantalizing spicy sauce, sandwiches of all types, and, of course, candy bars and chips. Thousands of straws, like tubular flags saluting the plastics industry, proudly poked up out of paper cups holding soda, beer, coffee, or maybe something stronger. Cigarettes dangled from the mouths of men and women, young and old. Tendrils of smoke filtered through my nose.

By luck or design, we had planted ourselves near the staging area of a parade that would last for what seemed like days and days, until our feet ached from standing on unyielding concrete. We dared not move from our vantage point, lest that hole close up and be lost forever. Sights, sounds, smells, and constant movement electrified the air. Anticipation was palpable. Immediately, our worldly cares slid right off our backs as easily as the copious sweat rolling its way down our spines. The California sun felt hot to us Midwesterners, even though it was not yet July.

In front of us were men dressed as women with big hair, perfect makeup, and high heels, which I couldn't imaging wearing to walk across the street, let alone for a whole parade. There were women in suits and leathers and women carrying whips, cracking the air with their chilling message. Power emanated from them like a subwoofer blasting its way into our tender eardrums. Shivers raced down my spine, joining the sweat already pooling there. That was all I cared to know about these women.

Rainbows of colors presented themselves everywhere. I wondered if the real rainbow was jealous of the most colorful scene I'd ever witnessed. It must have been thinking, *hmm, why didn't I think of that color?* Clothing, flags, scarves, socks, boots all carried rainbow themes throughout the parade. Muscled men walked by wearing not much more than rainbow-colored feathers. Muscles and feathers, feathers and muscles; a combination perceived by many to be an oxymoron, but it made a powerful presence.

"Are you catching all of this?" asked Ruthanne.

"Oh, yeah. It's quite a show and the real parade hasn't started yet, has it?"

"I don't think so, but just keep watching," she said.

I watched as lithe young men and women performed circus acts. "Queens" rode in convertibles, trying to perfect their wave. And oh, there was so much more. This was more drama, more promise, more anticipation than I'd ever before witnessed in my life. The excitement, the constant movement, the fluid activity, the seriousness, and yes, the contagious frivolity made my nerves jump all over the place. No Fourth of July parade would ever seem the same after this day.

The sidewalk behind us was a moving river of people, bold, brash, beautiful. I couldn't tell if these people were part of the parade or spectators getting into the spirit of things. They were no less colorful than what we were seeing in the street in front of us. This was the largest crowd I'd ever seen, a mass of thousands of people and certainly the largest parade I'd ever seen. Each entry formed to our left some blocks away, then moved slowly forward, following the command of some parade guru. They too, were waiting in anticipation, waving, smiling, and providing small acts of entertainment and engagement.

"Have you noticed a lot of these entries are supporters?" asked Ruthanne. "I saw PFLAG and several corporate signs. Those others must be local businesses."

"It's refreshing to see that kind of support. Maybe we're making progress."

"That's one way of looking at it. It's incredible, really," she mused.

"I think the whole town must be supporting this parade in one way or another."

I got lost in my thoughts, wondering how far some of these people had traveled to either be in or to watch this parade. We'd come from half a country away, not solely for the parade, but we were here nonetheless. Did people from other countries come too? It felt like it. There was a multitude of diversity, kind of like seeing our own little League of Nations right there on the streets of San Francisco. With that many people milling about, it was hard to say who was local and who wasn't.

Then, suddenly, moving to a spot right in front of us was a contingent I later learned was always the first to lead this glorious parade. A whole group of dykes on bikes. Big bikes. Big dykes. Lightning entered my head, zipped right down to my feet, then raced right back up to my heart, which was surely way too small to contain all this excitement. Those big dykes revved up those big bikes, revved up my pulse, revved up the whole crowd, and the crowd roared its approval. The bikes and their riders responded with even more enthusiasm. More revving. Lots of loud revving. Cheers settled on those dykes like food and water after a drought, and they drank it up. They were teasing us and we loved it. These women were anxious to get this parade started. I was anxious to do more than that with these women.

I studied these dykes on bikes as they tossed out confidence like confetti and waited for instructions to move forward. I expected to see some conformity to established modes of dress but found none whatsoever. Black leather gloves graced sturdy hands; sturdy hands gripped black rubber handlebars, tennis shoes contrasted with black knee boots, long hair opposed short hair. A few wore lipstick, but most didn't. Some women wore formal caps, remnants of some sort of uniform, others were bareheaded; some wore leather jackets.

Shorts, tank tops, sleeveless tops, some colorful, some not; it was all there. Women proudly presented themselves in every size and shape. Muscled arms and flabby arms waved to the eager crowd. These women followed no specific protocol, gay or straight, but marched to their own definition of womanhood. Dykes on bikes was this group's universal theme, but boldness emanated from them as if they'd been born on those big bikes and hadn't stopped riding them since.

Eventually, the parade actually started, and the dykes moved on like thunder accompanying a powerful storm. Their leaving left a settled quiet, but the zip I felt lasted the rest of the day. They enjoyed providing their entertainment and I enjoyed the entertainment they provided. What contingent came after them, I couldn't say.

We stayed for more entertainment until our feet, backs, hunger, and need to get farther north made us leave. We had room reservations in Weaverville, at least a five-hour drive, and needed to do our own moving on, albeit much more quietly.

"What time is it?" Ruthanne asked.

I glanced at my watch. Three hours had passed, yet it seemed like three minutes. "Geesh, it's one thirty already."

"We'd better go then. I think we parked that way," she said, pointing.

"We walked a couple of blocks before she asked, "Well, was that a good parade or what? Ruthanne always provides, doesn't she?"

"For sure, the best I've ever seen. It's too bad we can't watch the rest of it."

"Yeah, maybe next time."

We had stayed too long; we had not stayed long enough.

SAVING THE WORLD

Hey, Weaverville is having a parade while we are there.
Let's watch that and then we can hike the Coffee Creek
Trail and stay overnight at Hodges Cabin.

EMAIL FROM RUTHANNE TO PAT

"That cigarette stinks. Let's move back a bit," Ruthanne suggested. One sunny, breezy day we were standing around on a sidewalk in the small town of Weaverville, California, waiting for a summer parade to come by. I fully expected Ruthanne's comment about the smoker's inconsideration. If the man heard it, he didn't react. Totally unexpected, however, was that she didn't immediately say something to him.

Other people were milling about, chatting and sending frequent glances up the street in anticipation, as we were. For a small town whose business district was only a few blocks long, there was a sizeable crowd, but the sidewalks weren't so full that it was difficult to find a spot along the curb to await the big small-town event.

People were calm. The day was calm, warm but not hot. The clouds, what few of them there were, hung in the distant sky in layers, sort of like a ham sandwich. There would be no weather-related threat to these festivities. Everything predicted calm.

Then, nonchalantly, the man in front of us threw his cigarette butt into the street—still lit. Ruthanne's hackles rose. She snapped her head up, squared her shoulders, thrust out her chest, and donned her "save the world" armor. If she'd had long sleeves on, she'd have rolled them up. The heavy hiking boots, thankfully, were still in the car. With these preparations out of the way, she marched over and provided a grand performance for all to see. It wasn't technically a parade, but it was an impressive show.

The ball of her foot smashed that burning cigarette butt to miniscule particles with such force, it left a divot in the pavement. She took this job seriously, lest any portion escape and set the entire town on fire. Her whole body spoke volumes about her opinion of this man's littering. Littering with a lit cigarette butt in the dry California sun, in a town mere yards away from a vast wilderness. I think the sun actually blinked out for a few seconds. The earth merely shivered and kept on breathing.

I was even more surprised, though grateful, that she didn't turn to the man and say something equally endearing and colorful. Her actions, though, were loud and clear, easily interpreted by the most innocent of onlookers. *There, take that, you lazy, polluting oaf.*

Though I suspect *oaf* might not have been the word floating around in her head. It might just as well have come out of her mouth, but she remained silent.

The man wasn't quite so reticent. "You don't have to make such a big production of it," he said.

"The world is not your ashtray, and what you are doing is considered polluting. The rest of us don't appreciate it," she said quite calmly.

"It's my cigarette, and I can dispose of it however I want. It's a public place. It isn't just yours."

"No, it belongs to all of us, and you need to respect that."

"You just need to mind your own business." He turned his back to us, leaving the cigarette right where it lay—in millions of tiny pieces.

I already knew her feelings about smokers who felt free to throw their cigarette butts anywhere they pleased. When she spotted someone in a car throwing one out the window, she never failed to comment. "I wish I had a zapper when I see that. I'd zap them right in the back of the head. Maybe they would stop considering the world their ashtray."

Time stood still as she debated her next move. The sun kept smiling. The breeze moseyed along without a care in the world. The earth leaned back in a wait-and-see attitude. The nearby crowd waited patiently for both parades to start, hers and the official one. I could almost see the dilemma bouncing around in her brain as she stood stiffly staring at the man's back. It was like watching someone stand at the edge of a precipice. Will she, or won't she? The moment lingered while she stared holes in the back of that man's head. His posture said he was done with it. She opened her mouth, then immediately closed it, deciding to let it rest. She walked back to where I was nervously waiting. "Humans don't deserve this earth," she said.

How many times had I heard that before?

I'm not sure what others were thinking. I heard only the soft shuffling sounds of people slowly turning back to face the street. Were they disappointed, amused, startled?

Once the parade started, she showed every sign of enjoying it. There were the usual high school bands and themed floats. The expected Shriners' club wove in and out. But then another men's group, about eight or ten of them, came by riding toy stick horses. Ruthanne burst out with a laugh so sudden and forceful, I thought the people in front of her were going to fall over from the aftershock. Several turned to give her a brief curious look but said nothing. I knew then she was enjoying the world even if she wasn't able to save all of it.

EDMUND SPENSER'S CASTLE

Have you ever thought of going on an Earthwatch Expedition?

EMAIL FROM RUTHANNE TO PAT

"I don't know what that is."

"It's where volunteers work with researchers or other professionals to do something for the environment, like relocating turtle eggs or observing endangered animals or doing archeology digs. Or it could be conservation projects."

"What would we do?" I asked.

"Well, I can't go anywhere that's too hot because of my MS but I can do some research and come up with a few places for us to consider. I'll see if they have a catalog."

What she didn't tell me until later is that the volunteer pays for the project. That, plus the airfare, made it the expense equivalent of a ten-day vacation. And that's how she encouraged me to view it. A "working vacation," she called it. Since Earthwatch is a nonprofit organization, it was all tax deductible. Our fees helped fund the project and promote academic research.

"It's a way to give back," she said.

We chose Kilcolman Castle near Doneraile, Ireland, in County Cork. The castle remains are important because the poet Edmund Spenser spent a fair amount of time there sitting at a window bench writing his epic poem *The Faerie Queene*. His poem contained 4,000 stanzas and 36,000 lines, divided into six books, each with a different protagonist. It is one of the longest poems in the English language and became the source of the term Spenserian stanza.

The goal, according to lead researcher, Eric Klingelhofer, Ph.D., was to conduct an archaeological and architectural survey of Kilcolman Castle and its environs. We were to learn a great deal about castles, how they were built, and for what purpose. We were taught how to recognize additions or reconstruction efforts. Other lessons had to do with what they called the stringline, the murder hole, and a garderobe. What we did not learn too much about was the poet himself. Any learning in that direction was left up to us before or after the expedition.

Off we went, I with vacation time, and Ruthanne with the whole summer to waste since she had opted for a nine-month contract at her new teaching job. Because she had all that time, she decided to make a long vacation of it, leaving several days before I did and staying a week or so longer. The problem was figuring out how to find each other when it came time for the real purpose of our trip. I'd never flown by myself, let alone internationally. In the end, I flew into Ireland's Shannon airport and found my way to Tralee, a three-hour trip by bus.

I settled in my bus seat prepared for a long, boring trip, but the ride was incredible. The scenery flowing past my window was intensely colorful. The grass was such a deep rich green, I was sure they sprayed extra chlorophyll on it. Tiny little yards held amazing assortments of color, using both horizontal and vertical space for their creations. And the villages we went through were like colorful postcards with rows and rows of homes in every primary shade.

When I got to Tralee, I walked down the street, booked us a room for the night, and wandered around and found a grocery store. I bought a few snacks, though I was mostly choosing by the pictures on the package, not knowing what some of the words meant, even though they were English. With all that out of the way I did some more wandering and found a cool rose garden to waste time in. Lest I miss her bus, I went back to the bus station about a half hour early and waited for Ruthanne to arrive.

A funny thing happened during all my wandering and waiting around. I kept seeing all these people with freckles—just like me. *These are my people,* I thought. *Wow, this is amazing, these are my people.* My mother's people were from Scotland and my father's people from England, but these people were my kin. I was sure of it. They looked just like me.

The other cool thing is that I did all that on my own. I got to the Des Moines airport, made my airline connections, and ended up in Tralee right where and when I was supposed to be. It helped that we all spoke the same language, though there were times when I wasn't too sure of that, especially in Dingle. More than once, I stared at people's lips long after they quit speaking, in desperate hopes that what they said would somehow translate itself by the time it got to my ears. It amazed me too, that entering a store one day we encountered two young boys about seven or so speaking Gaelic to one another, but they greeted us in English. How did they know?

Never before had I made such a trip. But Ruthanne had faith in me, gave me a few tips, and off she went, fully expecting to see me at the expected place and time in good shape. After she arrived, we did a couple days of touristy things. Our first dinner should have been an omen to our culinary experiences during this trip. I ordered roast beef and vegetables. What I got was a boiled dinner, with the beef boiled to the point of no taste and the vegetables boiled beyond recognition, creating a kind of vegetable mush on the plate. It wasn't a very good introduction to the culinary status of Ireland.

At the second dinner I decided to order something the Irish knew how to cook—fish and chips. During that dinner, a French family sat a couple of tables away. The father and the son ate everything with abandon. The mother and the daughter ate only the dinner rolls and butter that came with whatever they had ordered. They refused to touch anything else, no matter how much their male companions encouraged them to eat more.

At a table closer to us sat a guy, presumably Irish, who ordered what we were to learn were called jacket potatoes. I would have thought that term meant baked, but out came a plateful of boiled potatoes with the skins still on. He was quite adept at removing the skins and eating only the fleshy part of the potato.

"Now why don't they remove those skins in the kitchen and make it easier for people to eat their dinner, I wonder."

"It's just the way the Irish do it, I guess," Ruthanne answered.

"If you're not going to eat the skin, why waste energy cooking it?"

She had no answer. Seeing those potatoes should have been another omen to our future culinary experiences.

After a couple of days, we met the rest of our Earthwatch group at a local pub, on July 5, 1993.

Just five days later, Irene, one of our leaders, told us that 50,000 people had been evacuated from downtown Des Moines because of a massive flood. Ruthanne laughed out loud.

"That would be more people than there are in downtown Des Moines, and more than a quarter of Des Moines' total population," she said.

It turned out to be more like 10,000 people evacuated, but it was still significant. Fortunately, we had someone checking up on our house, and she had everything under control, collecting good water for cooking and rainwater for other things.

We missed most of the flood's devastation, though I got home in time to experience a couple days without running water. Ruthanne had gone on from Ireland to Germany to visit Trudy, a woman she had worked with during her two years with the forest service in the Trinity Alps. She missed the entire flood.

Despite the news from home, we got on with our volunteer work. Our researcher, Eric, had three assistants, including Eamon, who was the only Irish representative in our whole crowd. Danny and Irene were on the scene too. They both admonished the rest of us that they did not want to hear us singing "Good Night, Irene" or "Oh Danny Boy."

Our leaders were all staying in local hotels, but found a two-hundred-year-old former nunnery for us volunteers to live in for the duration. It had four rooms, two up and two down. The smallest downstairs room had to be fitted with showers and toilets to accommodate these insane Americans who liked to bathe every day. They also hired a local cook to feed us.

Breakfast, as I recall, was simple; cereal of some sort. Lunch was a sandwich with lunch meat, or a meat spread, a scraping of butter, and three tiny watercress sprouts. I'm assuming the sprouts were there for decoration only. They added nothing to the flavor of the sandwich and probably very little nutrition. And that was it for leafy green vegetables. There were other things like fruit, chips, or cookies. It was the suppers that had all us Americans baffled. I don't remember the main courses, but there was a pot of boiled potatoes every night we were there. Boiled potatoes with the skins still on—jacket potatoes. At the end of each supper there were always at least half a dozen potatoes left over. Not knowing what else to do with them, we put them in the refrigerator.

Every day, we came down the hill from working at the castle to our lovely abode to find another big pot of boiled potatoes. The pile of leftover potatoes got higher and higher and higher, and we were eating fewer and fewer of them. They were filling up huge pans in the refrigerator. I, being the brave one, finally asked Eric if he could ask our cook to prepare us some other form of potato. Baked perhaps, or mashed, or scalloped.

"No," the cook said, startled out of her wits. "It's biling (boiling) season. Baking potatoes won't be ready for another month."

It was news to us that you couldn't take any ole potato and cook it however you felt like cooking it. The other volunteers said nothing and carried on just like the Irish advise.

In the meantime, that pile of potatoes kept growing until there were at least three dozen sitting in a big stock pot in the refrigerator. I asked Eric if we could possibly procure a dozen eggs. The next day we came down the hill to find eggs and more potatoes. The following morning, I got up early, chopped up a bunch of potatoes, fried them up and added all dozen eggs for a sort of homemade hash. When I set it on the table, the one Irish guy, Eamon, looked at them, turned up his nose, said "No, thanks," and walked into the other room. My eleven American friends scarfed them down with glee, tossing out accolades for me and giving thanks for something a bit different than the usual fare.

"You saved the day, Bootter," Ruthanne cooed.

"Yes, but what are we going to do with the mountain still in the fridge?"

I think we began tossing them into the woods behind our little house.

One person in our group asked if we could have a lettuce salad. The next night there was a small salad sitting on our table, but it disappeared in seconds. One brave soul asked if we could have a large enough salad that would serve twelve hungry people.

Again, sheer astonishment fell on our cook's face. "A salad that size would feed a family of five for a week in our country. We don't eat salads, we just put a little on the plate for decoration."

That was one of several cultural lessons we were to learn during our project. Towards the end of our stay, we were invited by people in the neighborhood to a backyard party. They wanted to hear all about our endeavors on behalf of their castle. Eric suggested we bring something to share. We had no problems with that, but not having a recipe book or a properly stocked kitchen we were in a dither. But then Ruthanne, with her excellent memory, wrote down the ingredients to make brownies. What she didn't do was write down how much of everything. She also didn't specify baking chocolate. Our cook took the list to town and came back with a slab of chocolate measuring about eight by twelve inches and about an inch and a half thick.

How much of this chunk do we use in one recipe of brownies? And then what do we do with the rest of it? We had no measuring implements, so the men of the group came up with an idea. Ruthanne told them how many ounces of chocolate the recipe called for. They used a transom we'd been using to survey the land—basically an eight-foot ruler, measured the chocolate, and commenced calculations.

Impatient with this nonsense, which was taking a while, Ruthanne used a pocketknife she always carried with her and scored a square along one corner of the slab.

"That's about how much we need," she said.

We began making our brownies and finally here came the guys. That giant measuring stick of theirs barely fit in the tiny kitchen, but they came in, leaned their giant ruler against the wall, had me hold the huge square of chocolate in place and used what looked like a hunting knife to cut off a square almost to the exact measurements Ruthanne had earlier marked. Men and their toys.

The oven knob had the numbers one through nine on it. Again,

Ruthanne, being practical, said we should choose a number in the middle and hope it's about 350 degrees Fahrenheit. It wasn't. When it came time to go to the party the brownies were partially done. We pushed the time as much as we could, but eventually had to take them out of the oven. We cut them, even the gooey ones in the center and placed them on a plate.

"Whatever you do," said Ruthanne, "put them at the back of the table. Maybe no one will notice them."

That backfired. I was standing near that very table when a woman came up and took a brownie.

"These brownies are great. How do you get them so nice and chewy?"

"Well," I said. "You start with a recipe from memory, contend with an oven whose markings are totally different than you're used to, run out of time, and serve them anyway. They're really a mistake and we shouldn't have brought them. They're underdone."

"Well, I think they're great," she said. "If no one else wants them, I'll have another."

"We put them at the back of the table for a reason," I said. "We're kind of embarrassed."

"More for me," she said.

One day our leaders decided to give us an afternoon off and drove us into the town of Mallow. I loved that little town. There was what they called the greengrocer, but there were a dozen or more little shops selling special items. There was a lamb shop, a smoke shop, a beef shop, a dessert shop and so on. We were told that, back in the day, this was how housewives got their news. They would visit all these little shops and pick up their food and whatever gossip there was to be had, and of course, share what they knew. I thought it was cool that there weren't superstores where you could buy your prom dress, your cowboy boots, your fine jewelry, and all your gardening supplies under one roof, in addition to your groceries. This was the way shopping was meant to be. It's so unlike our exhausting, super ego megastores selling stuff no one needs.

The other thing I noticed in Mallow was the ruins of a castle, and right across the street was a modern glass building. The old and the new sharing the same air space felt right to me. Enjoy the new but revere the old. What a cool concept.

I thoroughly enjoyed that work experience. I do need to give the Irish a fair shake as far as food is concerned. We found some wonderful food while there. Since then, I've read more than one article praising the new food revolution in Ireland. I want to go back to taste that. What was truly an Irish tradition, I think, was that no matter what we were working on, we stopped every morning and every afternoon for tea. We had real cups, a teapot, and containers of milk and sugar. There were biscuits as well but we call them shortbread cookies. We had a good time sitting around learning about each other's lives while having a nice tea break.

In the end, we left Ireland hoping someday to go back and spend more time touring. Unfortunately, Ruthanne didn't get to go again, and I'm still waiting for that opportunity.

FINDING KILCOLMAN

Thank you for your help at Kilcolman. We really could have used your attitudes and effort in the third group.

LETTER FROM IRENE TO RUTHANNE

This excerpt from Irene, one of our leaders, came later that summer. Apparently, they enjoyed us as much as we had enjoyed the expedition. I'd love to go back and see what progress they've made since then. Maybe we got a lot more done during that first session than the following two sessions. It really wasn't Edmund Spenser's castle; it's just where he had visited and where he wrote that epic poem. For a poem that long, he must have stayed for quite some time.

During those two weeks, we cleared quite a bit of overgrown vegetation, exposing masonry underneath. Ivy had grown unchecked for decades, if not centuries. Some of it was three inches thick, growing far out from the walls, and all of it accommodating decades of dust. We measured archeological details and used an old-fashioned transom to survey the surrounding landscape and lay a site grid. Final reports included topographical and geophysical survey results.

The first year was intended to provide enough data to begin archaeological excavations in subsequent years, and to locate a house

Sir Edmund Spenser apparently built there during the Elizabethan colonization period. We were the first of three teams to do this work that summer. Since it was for surveying purposes only, our tools consisted of hand-held trowels and rakes, and of course the survey tools. No shovels or real digging was allowed. Digging would come in later years, after the first year proved the site research-worthy.

I was assigned to tediously remove accumulated weeds and soil around an area on what we assumed was the backside of the castle. But one stone looked significantly different than all the rest I'd been seeing in that area. I can't explain why. It just looked different. Perhaps it spoke to me through the centuries. I went around the corner, trowel still in my hand, and asked Eric to come and take a look. As soon as he saw it, he took the trowel from my hand and began enthusiastically removing even more soil from around the stone. He was obviously intrigued by the possibility of finding something significant.

"I think we may have found the cornerstone," he said with excitement, and worked several more minutes on it. Pictures were taken and the excitement eventually died down. He gave my trowel back and we all carried on.

I still have pictures of Ruthanne and Karen, another volunteer, hanging precariously off the ledge of a window, trowels in hand, with their hooded jackets on backwards with the hood over their faces, essentially working blind. They should have had face masks on, but lacking that, it was the only way to keep from swallowing all the dust they were raising by pulling all that old ivy off.

There were teaching moments as well, each morning starting with a small lecture. We learned a great deal about castles and whether they were built for defense or habitation. Defensive castles in the 15th century had very narrow windows, making it more difficult for arrows, mortar shells, and other projectiles to enter the building, and the walls were often six to eight feet thick.

The walls in the old nunnery we lived in were eight inches thick and in the evenings we had to wear sweaters or jackets. Some of the perimeter stone walls around the property were built of two sets of walls, consisting of larger stones, with rubble rock tossed in between them, then the whole thing topped off with more stones. These were additional defensive structures, they said.

We learned about the twist of winding stairways. They were normally built to ascend to the right so that the person defending the castle could hold his weapon in his right hand and hold on to the wall with his left. The stairs in this castle were built to ascend to the left and we weren't sure why this was. Was the original owner left-handed? We learned the purpose of the murder hole: to pour hot grease on an intruder who had managed to get through all other defenses.

Eric discussed how to recognize the difference between the original structure and any additions in subsequent years or decades. We knew these things by the type of mortar used and the difference in the type of stones used.

The garderobe is what I would call an indoor/outdoor toilet. It looked like an afterthought addition to the original structure; the stone structure abuts the original castle walls but is not integrated. On the outside, picture a wide chimney attached to the side of the building. At the bottom, and up about four feet from the ground, was a "cleanout" hole to allow easy removal of all the accumulated "stuff." On the inside, and on the second floor, inside this chimney-like room, there was a stone plank with a hole cut in it. Quite primitive, with minimal comforts. It was called a garderobe because users were cautioned to "guard your robe" while using these crude facilities, which may not have been all that clean.

All those measurements we took were to be fed into a computer, which would organize it and possibly indicate where buried structures like walls, drains, pits, or other interesting items lay.

Judy wrote in a Christmas card about *memories of a most unusual two weeks of my life. It seems really fun as I look back but think at the time it felt on the edge of maddening.*

Ruthanne and I found the whole experience interesting. I don't think either of us found it maddening. We saw it as a big learning adventure, and that's pretty much what it turned out to be. Other than having boiled potatoes every blessed day, we had a grand time. We met nice people, saw some of the countryside, and had some incredible food after the expedition was over. Ruthanne and I found a woman who prepared meals in her own home. She served Ruthanne a wonderful salmon dinner and me a nice pork chop. We were happy.

We liked the country, and we liked the people. On our first day there, we asked someone for directions to the visitor's center. She started to give us directions then said, "Well, I'll just take you there." And she did, walking us all the way down the street, turning the corner, and pointing across the street.

Someday, I hope to revisit one of the greenest, friendliest places I've ever been.

CARDBOARD OVENS

Have you ever felt that even though you're taking things one day at a time…it's about twenty-four hours more than you can take?

AMBASSADOR CARD FROM PAT TO RUTHANNE

I agree with the sentiments in this card, but at least *I get to come out and see you in a week and a half. It will be good to spend some time with you.*

Ruthanne was still on the job with the forest service, and I accompanied her on a couple of her hikes into the mountains. One of those places was quite isolated and there was a youth group up there, about a two-hour hike.

"These kids are here because there are some issues going on in their lives," Ruthanne warned me. "The leaders are really nice. I'd like to check up on them if you don't mind."

"Sure," I said.

I became a Girl Scout leader when my oldest daughter Glori was in first grade. I had no idea of the fun and useful things I would learn during new leader training. Besides songs and games, or arts and crafts, there was all sorts of outdoor skills training. I learned how to cook stuff in a paper sack, a paper cup, aluminum foil, on a dingle stick, on a tripod, in a hole in the ground, and lots of other ways. Cooking anything outdoors was my idea of a good time.

These outdoor skills became my favorite. I learned how to use, maintain, and store equipment like cast iron cookware, lanterns, shovels, and rakes. I wish I still took care of my own hand tools like I did theirs. I was out in my tool shed the other day and thought, *you need to invite a group of Girl Scouts over to help you take care of your tools.*

There is a fire for almost any situation, and the fire one builds needs to fit the cooking situation. When I became Association Chair, I conducted monthly meetings for about thirty other leaders in a church basement. I always saved the last fifteen minutes of each meeting for a mini-training session. They might learn some of the skills already mentioned or other useful leader type skills.

One day I took a stack of wood with me and demonstrated about six different types of fires, showing the leaders everything except lighting them. During that session there was one leader who had her four-year-old son with her as she always did at these meetings. He was quiet, well behaved, and spent the entire meeting never speaking or causing any kind of trouble. About two weeks after this particular mini-training the mother called me.

"I wanted to tell you what my son did the other day. He was in the back yard playing and became so quiet that I thought I should go check up on him."

"Did he leave the yard?" I asked.

"No, we have a very long yard with a shed at the far end and a wood pile right next to it. He had assembled all six of the fires you demonstrated at the meeting the other day."

"All of them?"

"Absolutely, and he did a pretty good job of it. He had them all laid out the way you demonstrated. I didn't know he was paying that much attention."

"Good for him. I'm glad he got so much out of it."

"Good for you. He copied everything you did perfectly."

I was a bit proud. Not knowing whether any of the adult learners got that much out of it, I took my accolades where I could get them. I went on teaching other people many of those skills I had learned, eventually becoming a trainer myself.

I cringe when I see people building huge fires to roast a hot dog over. In fact, I really cringe when I see people cooking over fire at all. "They need to be cooking over coals, not fire," I said out loud to Ruthanne many times.

She didn't believe in using wood fires at all. She thought it depleted our natural resources. I've planted enough trees in my life to more than make up for all the wood I've used in outdoor fires. And I see it as a renewable source, so long as you don't burn more than you replace.

She did approve of the cardboard box oven. Before you can use one, you have to assemble the thing, which is cool too. You use what you make. You make what you use.

You start with two cardboard boxes with the tops still attached on at least one side. Cut one box apart, trim the pieces, wrap the pieces in heavy duty aluminum foil and insert them into the other box in their respective places, taping the top piece to the underside of the lid. I took my cardboard oven on many camping trips and enjoyed baked biscuits, potatoes, and chicken, as well as teaching family members how to bake in it. For our backpacking trips, I worked with one box oven for days until I figured out a way to make it collapsible and easily packable. It was nice to have biscuits or a baked potato with our backpacking fare. And it was lightweight and easy to carry.

When I went back to school as an adult, I had to take the dreaded speech class, and bombed out on my first speech. Next was to be a demonstration speech. Fearing another failure, I bemoaned my predicament. Always a solution finder, Ruthanne suggested the cardboard oven. My box oven was the perfect item. I got up early and baked biscuits in my oven, then packed everything up, got to class, handed the treats out and showed the class how to assemble and properly use the oven. Not only did I get an A for that speech, but after class two students came up to me and asked, "Do you have written instructions for making this oven?"

"No," I said, "But I can create some if you'd like."

"Thanks, that would be great," they replied.

"I'll bring them to the next class," I told them.

Perhaps I should have turned that paper in for a composition class. I have to admit it pleased me that others were interested in something so close to my heart.

But on this mountain, with the youth group, we were sitting around chatting when Ruthanne asked, "How do you manage to cook for this crowd?"

One of the adult leaders said, "We do well enough on the open fire. We do a lot of frying and/or boiling, and sometimes roast things on a stick, but we mostly serve lots of one pot meals."

"Do you ever bake things?" Ruthanne asked.

"How would we do that without an oven? I'd love to bake potatoes or something."

Ruthanne jumped on that idea right away. "Pat can teach you how to do that. She's taught all kinds of people how to make an oven out of cardboard boxes."

"Really?" was the incredulous reply of one leader.

"And you can actually bake in it?" asked another.

"We'd have to have some basic supplies," I said. I wasn't sure we could round up everything we needed, though Ruthanne thought I could perform miracles.

I listed the minimum we would need, and they scrounged around and came up with most of it. We assembled a fairly nice, serviceable box oven. Fortunately, they had packed much of their supplies up there in cardboard boxes. They only had regular aluminum foil instead of heavy duty, and masking tape instead of duct tape. But we made do. After it was done, I demonstrated how to use it and instructed them on how to improve on it once they could get proper supplies.

"Now remember," I said, "one charcoal briquette equals about 40 to 50 degrees of heat, so you can calculate how many you need for the temperature you want. If you are using coals from a wood fire, remember not to overdo it. It's better to take longer to cook at a lower temperature than to burn everything to a crisp with too much heat. And remember to put the ventilation holes near the bottom, or one of two things will happen. Without vent holes, either your food will taste like smoke, or with a lack of air flowing through the box, your coals will die out before the food is cooked."

After that, I gave them a short lesson on the three requirements for building a fire: fuel, oxygen, and an incendiary device. That would include matches, magnified sun, flint, or coals from a previous fire.

Shortly after that, Ruthanne and I left. I never knew how that group's cooking skills with their new box oven turned out. I always wished we could have gone back up there for another visit to see how they were getting along. But I have to assume they did all right with the lessons they got, and a working oven too.

BEE TREE GAP

Great news. Barb and Connie will be going on the TAWGA [Trinity Alps Women's Get Away] trip with us.

EMAIL FROM RUTHANNE TO PAT

The sun blazed high in the sky by the time we reached the trailhead. Its scorching breath sucked ours right out of our lungs the moment we stepped out of the car. A glance at the sky revealed three wispy, miniscule clouds, miles away. I felt my skin drying up right on the spot. My watch said 11:00 already, and here we were about to embark on what would become an all-day hike.

"We need to be at the trailhead no later than eight tomorrow morning. Earlier if we can." Ruthanne said the night before.

She knew something we didn't. No one said a word because no one else understood the significance of the order. Connie and Barb hadn't hiked in the Trinity Alps in northern California before and didn't understand the need to start the day early. I had hiked several of those trails—Swift Creek, Coffee Creek to Hodge's Cabin, Long Trail, and others.

But most of them had a fair amount of tree canopy, providing a nice mixture of sun and shade. Just when you don't think you can take any more sun, nature provides a few trees with their delicious inviting coolness underneath. And just when the shade, and any breeze accompanying it, starts to chill the sweat on your body, the sun seems like a great idea again. It becomes a beautiful dance of nature from trailhead to destination. Nature never lets you become too complacent. And it almost always provides just what you need just when you need it.

What the rest of us didn't know was that the trailhead was at 3,800 feet and the climb would take us another 3,400 feet up. Trail guides suggest allowing six hours, but it took us eight. Had three of us known that at the beginning, we might have protested.

That trail was straight up with one level spot. This only level spot also had a few trees growing in it. Some stones and downed tree trunks provided sitting spaces. It truly was an oasis in the midst of this inferno. The moment we walked into it we noticed a drop in the temperature. It felt twenty degrees cooler in there and was a huge relief from the sun. We had a leisurely lunch there. But the moment we left, we felt sorry to leave it behind. Ruthanne had hiked this trail previously and knew that none of us wimps would make it to the top with full packs on our backs, but I think she still overestimated our abilities. I wished we could camp there for the night, but the horses were already on the way to the very top of the mountain with the rest of our gear. If I'd had a large rope, I would have asked the horses to drag that oasis to the top for us.

Ruthanne didn't like our rest periods to last more than five minutes, but this one lingered closer to a half hour. None of us wanted to move from that shade, knowing what awaited us.

"We can't sit here all day," Ruthanne finally said. "We'd best get moving. We have a long way to go."

That was an understatement. We moved on, but anyone who has ever hiked Bee Tree Gap will tell you, there is nothing between you and the California sun in those open spaces. The sun kept on smiling, sharing its intensity, and reminding us to drink plenty of water, lest we fall into a giant dust heap right there on the trail. At the end of any hike, Ruthanne always said, "I want you to keep drinking water until you pee. That way I will know you are fully hydrated again."

She gave us our instructions the night before. "Tomorrow, you will want to pack a full bottle of water, a jacket, sunscreen, hat, reading material, snacks, and lunch in your day packs. One of us will carry a water filter. The rest we will let the horse packers carry."

I was assigned to carry the water filter. Ruthanne always carried the first aid kit, housed in a bright orange stuff sack for easy and quick identification. We dispensed with the rest of our gear at the horse packer's home the night before, just after we had gotten the "early start" advisory from Ruthanne.

A few hours into the hike I began to appreciate those horses. They were at the top of my hero list that day. I couldn't imagine our small group hauling two tents and their accompanying tent flies and ground cloths, cooking gear for four people, two days' food supply, four sleeping bags and sleeping pads, eating utensils, personal hygiene products, clothing, flashlights, extra water containers, and a whole host of other stuff up that mountain. Even with four of us sharing the load, it would have been too much.

On occasion, Ruthanne would carry a surprise treat in her pack for the entire hike and then produce it at the end of the day when everyone was just sitting around chatting. It might be candy, or a box of cookies, or a bottle of wine. Having been on several of Ruthanne's hiking trips, I knew her special treats were produced at the end of the day, and I wondered what the treat would be at the end of this hike to Bee Tree Gap. *It had better be a humdinger,* I thought.

On another Trinity Alps hike, we took along a boxed dessert containing the ingredients for a graham cracker crust, a sumptuous cream cheese filling, and a nice topping layer. We assembled it in an aluminum pan, put a nice tight lid on it, put it in a zip lock bag, tied a rope around it, and slid it into the creek, tying the other end of the rope to a small tree. A few hours later, the rope helped us retrieve it, and it came out looking as if it had been indoors in the refrigerator all day long. Nature always provides. The only problem was that the dessert was an eight-portion serving and there were but four of us eating it. Where were all those teenage hikers we'd seen the day before? It was tough eating all that in one sitting, but it was a fulfilling ending to that particular day.

We kept doggedly trudging up that mountain, thinking it would be weeks before we got to the top. Don't get me wrong. There were some interesting times on that arduous hike as well. "Every hour we need to take a five-minute break," Ruthanne instructed.

"That's all?" someone chirped.

"Any more than ten minutes and you'll find it extremely difficult to motivate yourself to get back up and begin hiking again. And no matter how much you want to, do NOT take your boots off. Believe me, you'll never want to put them back on again."

I already knew that was true from all the hikes I'd taken with her in the past. Once we hiked the Horseshoe Lake and Ward Lake loop, taking a leisurely two days getting there. Unwisely, we decided to do the entire descent in one day. It was all downhill, right? When we got back to the trailhead, we took our boots off and immediately discovered our mistake. Our feet throbbed so much I felt every heartbeat and every pulse for the next three hours. I didn't know feet could hurt like that.

You couldn't have paid either one of us to put those boots back on. We tender footed it across dirt, gravel, and tree roots to get back to the car. We tossed those boots in the trunk, put tennis shoes on, found a motel, filled the tub with cool water and sat on the edge, soaking our feet until all that throbbing ceased. We looked like two birds sitting on a telephone wire passing the time of day, but that water felt so good.

On this hike to Bee Tree Gap, I noticed after each one of these five-minute breaks—that sometimes stretched quite a bit longer, despite Ruthanne's urging to get moving—all four of us jockeyed for last position in the line of hikers. I understood why the leader of the pack wants to relinquish the head of the line occasionally. That's the person who gets all the cobwebs in the face, trying desperately to dance their way out of it, though that happens mostly in wooded areas. Cobwebs weren't an issue on this hot, treeless day. "Go ahead," I said to Barb after one of these breaks.

"No, you go ahead," she said. "I like being last."

"I've noticed. Why is that?"

"You don't know?" she asked incredulously. "The last one in line can fart all they want and not bother anyone else, and not have to be saying excuse me all day."

"Aha," I said with a chuckle and let her take the last position. It made me extra cautious about staying far enough ahead of her so that I too had my freedom.

There were plenty of big rocks and boulders to sit on during our breaks. Rocks that had been sitting in the hot California sun all day and practically fried the skin on the back of our legs as we sat down. Sometimes those rocks were big enough to lie down on, giving about two minutes' respite. Accommodating, but not comfortable.

We began soaking our "all-purpose rags," as Ruthanne called them, in water and tying them around our necks, cowboy style. An all-purpose rag, often verbally shortened to APR, can be any cotton material, but we used those large bandanas you see in every western movie. They were nicknamed "all-purpose" because they could also be used as a hot pad holder, wash cloth, a headband, a sweat wipe, a bandage or tourniquet in emergencies, a miniature tablecloth, an emergency signal on the end of a stick, and lots of other unique uses.

Later rest stops found us soaking our hats in a nearby cool stream. As the day wore on, this helped for a few minutes at best. I never did see steam coming from my hiking mates' hats, but they dried out within a half hour of each soaking. So much for that technique for staying cool.

We were using water for both drinking and cooling, running through our supply like it was infinite, so the water filter was one of the most important pieces of equipment. I'd give up my tent or sleeping bag before I'd give up a good water filter.

Ruthanne had lots of rules about conservation: leaving the environment cleaner than we found it, no open fires in the wilderness, take only pictures, carry everything out. But she always made sure we had plenty of good clean drinking water on any hiking trip, and the only time I remember being extravagant with water was a trip to Morris Meadows. We bought a bag made of about eight-mil plastic, black on one side, measuring 16 inches by 20 inches with a hose and nozzle attached to it. It gets filled with water from the creek and placed in the sun, black side up, for several hours. When it's hung in a tree, it becomes a useful shower in the wilderness. It was a nice luxury, but more difficult than useful.

About six hours into our hike to Bee Tree Gap, nature once again provided the best respite ever, though it took us a while to appreciate the gift. "Is that snow I see up ahead?" asked Connie.

"Yes," replied Ruthanne, "and it concerns me."

"Why? It's just snow," I said.

"It looks deep, and it could obscure the trail. It's too late in the day to be losing the trail for any length of time."

When we got nearer, we stopped to survey the situation. "Now what?" I asked.

"Well," said Ruthanne, "we carefully pick our route and hope we don't lose the trail too much. I don't see any trail markers nearby. Let's hope we find one soon."

And we did just that, finding the trail again after about an hour. But on the way through all that, someone had a bright idea. We began filling our hats with snow and putting them back on our heads. I had melting snow pouring down my face and neck, but I did not care. I made snowballs and rubbed them on my arms, face, and neck. The snow in the hat didn't last long. Neither did the snowballs, but the snow was plentiful. The irony of walking in shorts and t-shirts through knee-deep snow while sweating profusely wasn't lost on any of us.

At some point we encountered the horses coming down the mountain we were still trying to climb. Dee, the guy who owns Trinity Outfitters, was in the lead and stopped to talk to us for a while. They apparently left at a decent hour of the morning because they had reached the top, left our stuff, and were more than halfway down the mountain when we encountered them. "Here, I'll bet you folks would like one of these," he said as he pulled four cans of deliciously cold soda pop out of a cooler the horses were packing.

"Oh, thank you," the four of us said adoringly, every one of us putting the cans to our foreheads before opening them and taking a long swig.

"We left your stuff near a clump of trees in the meadow."

Ruthanne said "thanks," like she knew exactly what that meant. I didn't think anything of it because we hadn't seen a single tree since we left the oasis. I figured there would be a wide-open expanse of space, and there in the middle of it would be our gear in a meadow. I envisioned something like a football field with a large pile of stuff in the middle.

We trudged on, taking our five-minute breaks by sitting on more rocks hot enough to bake bread. We drank warm water from our bottles and ate tons of GORP to fuel us for the next jaunt.

GORP has several meanings. Some say it is an acronym for Good

Ole Reliable Peanuts, and others say it means Good Ole Raisins and Peanuts. Early dictionaries defined it as "to eat greedily." For us, GORP was copious amounts of Cheerios cereal with lots of other protein and energy-boosting ingredients. After eating that much cereal, we all noticed, and commented on, the difference in our bathroom habits the next day. It's amazing what scientific discoveries one experiences in the wilderness.

And speaking of bathrooms, usually we carried a trowel with us and dug a hole whenever we needed it, then covered it up. With the number of people hiking in these areas, you can imagine how many of these one-use holes there are all over the place. I'm surprised I've never accidentally stepped in one. On one hike, I sneaked up a rocky cliff and found some huge flat rocks that to me looked like a good place to sit and do one's duty. Behind one of them, I painstakingly dug a shallow pit, carefully reserving the excavated dirt beside the hole, stabbed the trowel into the pile, and proudly showed my creation to my hiking mates. Ruthanne asked, "What are you going to do with it when we leave here?"

"Fill the hole back in," I replied, disappointed at her lack of enthusiasm for my creation.

"It's pretty close to the trail, but at least it's on the other side of the rocks," she complained.

Eventually, after eight long, tortuous, blistering hot hours of hiking, we came to Bee Tree Gap, though we only knew that because there was a miniscule sign saying so. We almost missed it, since it was tacked high up on a tree trunk and was no larger than an index card. After a hike like that, there should have been fireworks greeting us. If not for the sign we might have hiked several more hours.

Once we got there, we had to admit the scenery was great, but there were lots of trees, and we didn't see our gear. We were baffled and turned several complete circles, looking near and far for our pile. After a couple of minutes, we decided to spread out and look in different directions.

"Don't go too far, though," admonished Ruthanne. She wasn't about to take a chance on losing us now. She needn't have worried. Our exhaustion was so great, the last thing any of us wanted was to walk some more.

The direction I took was downhill. I walked a few feet and came to what looked like a narrow irrigation ditch full of water. I turned and went to the left, and within three feet found another ditch. This pattern covered about fifty feet, making it hard to get anywhere. I guess they were nature-made gullies coming down the mountain.

Connie went uphill, and Barb moved farther along a path meandering on through the campsite and beyond.

"I've got it," Ruthanne yelled. Once we were back together, she started barking out orders. "I know it seems like we have lots of daylight left, but once that sun sets it gets real dark real fast. The tents go up first. Always shelter first, then food."

I agreed with her on this, because all my armchair reading about outdoor survival said so. Shelter from the elements is most important. This is especially true if time is an issue as it was that day.

Looking up the hill, Ruthanne pointed to a faraway spot and said, "The latrine will be up there near those two bushes." The latrine is always at least a hundred yards away from cooking, sleeping, and water sources. Since we were literally on the side of a sloping mountain, with our campsite at the lower end, she chose a spot about two hundred yards away. At least it did provide some measure of privacy, along with more exercise we didn't need at that point in the day.

Two people were assigned to pitching tents, one to filtering enough water for cooking and drinking, and one to find all the gear and necessary food to begin cooking supper. We were all hot, tired, and in bad moods. Well, three of us were anyway. Ruthanne kept her thoughts to herself. The last thing any of wanted was to work. But we silently did our assignments because we knew it was necessary. At one point I walked past Barb and said, "I'm so hot and tired, I just want to sit down for the rest of the evening."

"Hot and tired?" she said, "I'm approaching grumpy."

"Approaching?" I asked. "I've been grumpy for the last four hours."

We got the work done, had a nice supper, and sat around the rest of the evening enjoying reading and watching the gorgeous sky with all of its glittering stars. Looking back at it now, I think we could have shaved an hour or more from that hike had we made our breaks shorter as Ruthanne had advised. But those breaks provided lots of valuable conversation time.

As predicted, Ruthanne produced the evening treat: a big package of Oreo cookies. I normally don't like Oreos, but I, like everyone else, scarfed them down. We reduced those cookies to crumbs inside of fifteen minutes, despite having had an adequate, if boring, supper. I'm sure we were all thinking, "Hey, I need the calories."

Eight hours of hiking uphill consumes enormous calories. Some hikers carry, as Ruthanne did on the Appalachian Trail, squeeze bottles of fake butter, explicitly for the extra calories. It's liberally squirted into and onto everything they eat. We used that goo when we hiked in the Adirondacks, not quite as arduous as Bee Tree Gap, but certainly a good day's work. A mountain is a mountain. Exhilarating when you arrive, but hard work all the way up.

The next day we gathered our day packs with all the requisite gear, set them aside while we tackled striking the tents, put all the gear back into stuff sacks, filled our water bottles, and left the campsite on the opposite side to hike down the other side of the mountain.

Again, the day was hot, but we were almost giddy to be going downhill, despite our protesting knees, and we made good time. After a couple of hours, we came to a small lake and decided it was a good stopping spot. Ruthanne disrobed and swam the diameter; Barb disrobed and swam the perimeter. Connie and I sat on hot rocks and read awhile.

Ruthanne and Barb joined us, and we spent about an hour taking it easy. The only problem was that unrelenting sun. The sweat began to pour off us. This time though, the environment provided us with trees. It took about ten minutes for the sun to send us to the comfort of the trees and their luxurious shade. It took about ten more minutes for the shade to start cooling our skin enough to give us genuine chills. That was hard to believe after all the sweating we'd done the day before. Thus, began our slow waltz with the sun and the shade, the shade and the sun. Back and forth we went for about an hour. But we were immensely grateful to have both sun and shade within close proximity, and that they were such good friends, cohabiting quite nicely. We made no complaints. Nature always provides.

ETERNAL QUESTIONS

She needs to state the message and then stop talking.

COMMENT FROM CAROL TO PAT AFTER
RUTHANNE LEFT A VERY DETAILED VOICEMAIL

Ruthanne could go into great detail about the most mundane subjects. Wyatt, our second grandson, perhaps seven or eight years old at the time, asked her to explain the concept of investing. At the end of that thirty-minute lesson, which he swears was two hours long, all Wyatt could say was "Oh."

On a car trip with Ruthanne's grandmother Emma, we had a similar experience. "What's the difference between Lutherans and Methodists?" Emma asked.

We drove from Harmony in the southeast corner of Minnesota almost to Minneapolis by the time Ruthanne closed up shop on that answer. She explained the system of confessions, church structure, belief systems, governance style, sacraments, parishioner expectations, and how each church viewed original sin. I was impressed with Ruthanne's amazing recall of a class on comparative religions taken eons ago. Perhaps she thought it would be easier for Emma to remember, and the questions would stop.

Heck, I wasn't remembering most of this stuff. But like Wyatt, I knew not to ask more questions.

I knew then that Ruthanne was in the wrong profession. She was a good teacher, but the FBI would have loved her. She knew the minutest details about many things and had no trouble articulating any of it. They could have sent her out on a fact-finding mission and then wait for her to come back with a complete dossier on the subject. And not one word of it would have been in printed form. All she would have had to do was open her mouth and let the information all fall out while they watched in awe. Many of our friends have done the same, thoroughly amazed at the stuff she knew about so many subjects. Some asked me, "How does she know so much?" and others asked, "Are you getting all this?" assuming I was recording everything she said.

The problem was Emma had Alzheimer's. Wyatt did not. He knew not to ask any more tough questions. Ten minutes after Ruthanne's first answer, Emma asked the question again. Sometimes, smart as Ruthanne was, she was slow on the uptake. She launched into another long explanation of the differences between Lutherans and Methodists, possibly cutting two minutes off her previous answer.

Ten minutes later the question came again. With a big sigh, Ruthanne started again. If the first two answers were novels, this was a novella. She cut out the church structure, the governance style, and the sacraments, but hit hard on the theological differences. After that, we tried to develop a different conversational route, but here came the question again. This time Ruthanne dropped all but the theology, condensing the novella to a short story.

Regular as clockwork, Emma posed the question again. It amazed me how this elderly person could remember the question long enough to ask it repeatedly but could not remember ever having heard the answer. Yet, she could still play the piano. Emma never learned to read music, but she only needed to hear a song once to be able to play it.

Even with Alzheimer's she could still play. Ruthanne made a notebook for the nursing home to use when Emma wanted to play. It listed more than 130 songs she could play by ear. But that's a long-term memory function. Short-term memory was the issue on this day.

The Enriched Living Blog (ELB) says short-term memories are stored in the hippocampus until being sent to long-term memory. The problem arises because the hippocampus is the first brain function to deteriorate with Alzheimer's, therefore new memories never get permanently stored. Think of it, ELB says, as "last in, first out." That lesson proved itself to be true on a visit to Emma several months earlier, when Ruthanne laughed out loud.

"You sound just like my granddaughter Ruthanne," Emma said.

"I am your granddaughter, Ruthanne," she replied with a chuckle.

"You are?"

Emma didn't recognize the person in front of her, but she recognized that laugh from a time and place before Alzheimer's. That's what the disease does to brains. Emma had, at that point, outlived all four of her children. When she asked us how Ruthanne's dad was, we made things easy for her. "Oh, he's about the same as last time."

A true statement if lacking a few details, like his death a few years before that. I did think that had I outlived all my children and had to depend on grandchildren to take me places, I too, might have slipped into another dimension.

Ruthanne always met Emma in whatever state of mind she was in. When Emma mentioned that she and Helmer, her late husband, would be coming down to visit us sometime soon, Ruthanne let her know that we would be looking forward to it. There's no point in disturbing an already disturbed mind.

The next time Emma posed the Lutheran/Methodist question, Ruthanne opted for the short-answer version, covering just the basics. For a while I thought we were in a Kafka novel with no end in sight. I almost slipped her a note saying, *She's not getting any of this.*

Finally, Ruthanne got it, and the next time, gave a relatively brief statement of faith and theology. Again, came the question, and a shorter answer. I think we played this game a total of seven times and the answers got increasingly shorter. By the sixth time, Ruthanne had her answer down to a two-sentence synopsis. Not only was her recall in excellent shape, but also her ability to condense truly amazed me. I didn't know she could do that.

By the last time, I was truly proud of her tenacity, patience, and finally, extreme brevity, cutting even the synopsis down to a bare minimum.

"What's the difference…?" came the question for the seventh time that day.

Ruthanne's answer: "Not much."

MY BRIEF JOURNEY

Ortha went to an appointment with me. She expected me to be weepy, upset, worried, full of angst. You know how well I do that nonsense.

LETTER FROM PAT TO RUTHANNE

In late August of 1998 we were hiking in the mountains of Maine where I was experiencing extreme fatigue—a new phenomenon for me. Ruthanne had Multiple Sclerosis and lived with chronic fatigue daily. I finally knew how she felt. I had taken my lessons from Ruthanne and just kept on moving no matter how tired I felt. Oddly, I thought perhaps it was my lack of technique. Ruthanne had taught me years before how to do the rest step. It saves your muscles from the next day's excruciating pain after this day's overexertion. It works whether you're climbing mountains or a long flight of stairs.

But on second thought, I realized it wasn't my laziness. I was truly exhausted. This fatigue wasn't like I might feel after hiking all day, or after a morning at the gym. It felt more like anemic fatigue, which, as it turned out, was the case. We just hadn't figured that out yet. About a week after we came home, I got up about 3:00 a.m. and just as I was leaving the bathroom, I fainted. My fall brought Ruthanne out of a deep sleep and into the bathroom. The next thing I remembered was hearing her call my name a couple of times.

"What happened?"

"Never mind, it's obvious you fainted." She helped me get up and suggested I go back to bed "while I straighten things out in here."

I fainted again on the way back to the bedroom, hitting my head on the hall light switch on the way down. Rushing out to the hallway, she said, "I'm sorry, I didn't realize you were that weak. This isn't right. I'm calling the doctor. But first, let me get you back to bed."

Doctor Honsey was straightforward. "If she's fainted twice in succession, she has no blood pressure. You need to take her to the emergency room."

We went, they performed several tests, and we went back home. No one gave us any diagnosis or any suggestions as to why I had fainted. It seemed that was the end of it, and I resumed my life as usual.

Several days later, I took Ruthanne to the airport. She was to fly to London and then find her way to Cambridge to begin her fall semester of teaching abroad. She wouldn't be home until early December. The next day, Friday, after work, I was to drive to Cedar Rapids to spend the weekend with Ruthanne's mother, Ortha. I got home at 4:00 and was about to take my suitcase to the car when the phone rang. It was the doctor who had examined me in the emergency room, and she launched right in. "You have endometrial cancer."

Most of what she said after that, I didn't hear. My very first thought was, *I'm not going to see two-year-old Jarrett grow up or meet any other grandkids my daughters will eventually give me.* I remembered the last time I visited Jarrett and how excited he was to see me. There would be no more days at the park or weekend visits with his nanas. He wouldn't have many more chances to sit on my lap while I read books to him. There wouldn't be any more cookie making days or whimsical pictures drawn with sidewalk chalk. I was distressed that I wouldn't see how he turned out as an adult or what kind of kid he would be growing up. I waited a long time for grandkids; now this.

With these thoughts running through my mind, I missed the next several things the doctor said to me, but I did hear her say, "You can also go to Iowa City or Mayo Clinic for treatment." I associated both of those venues with serious cases. Hearing those two options meant to me a death sentence, and it was apparently imminent. Mostly, I thought, *if she's suggesting I leave Des Moines for treatment, it must be really bad.*

After our conversation, ninety percent of which I missed, I tried to get my mind back to working order. I needed to get on the road. I needed to pull myself together for the weekend. Still, I sat for another half hour trying to make sense of my world. Self-made predictions piled one on top of another. My mind was racing, my body was dithering. *What the heck am I supposed to do now?* I asked myself. No answers came, but loads of questions kept coming, racing to be the most important and first in line, yet making no real traction in my decision-making skills.

I needed to talk to Ruthanne but had no way of reaching her. I needed to get in the car and drive two hours to spend the weekend with someone who was not going to be the first person to get this news. Ortha's husband, Ruthanne's father, had died just over a year earlier. Just after his diagnosis, he asked the family not to tell anyone yet, because he wanted time to think about his options and what the rest of his life would look like. He also wanted to tell people about his disease in his own time and his own way. As luck would have it, they had already scheduled a party for the following week after his diagnosis and decided to go ahead with it. By the end of that party, Ortha had told that news to everyone present. She made the illness all about her and was already garnering sympathy from all who would give it. I lost a little respect for her that night. I was determined not to have that happen to me. My story was going to be told where, when, and to whom I decided—Ruthanne first.

How am I going to get through this weekend? I wondered.

I really didn't want to go but thought it might raise red flags if I didn't. So, I dragged myself up out of the chair and out to the car. I went to Ortha's and spent the rest of that evening worrying about how I was going to get the message to Ruthanne, without her mother hearing the conversation. I knew Ruthanne was scheduled to call us later that evening, and she did. Miraculously, Ortha said, "Well, I suppose you two want to talk alone."

I took the phone into the bedroom and shut the door. Because I was afraid of being overheard, I didn't say anything about the diagnosis. I said, "Call me on Sunday night at home."

"Why, what's going on?" she asked.

"Just call me, okay? I need to talk to you alone," I whispered into the phone.

The rest of that weekend was torturous. I spent an eternity worrying. My jittery mind was spinning, anxious, still making judgments about my future. My body was present, but my mind was all over the place with precious little of it residing in the same room. At some point Ortha said, "You're awfully quiet."

"I just miss Ruthanne already," I answered.

I didn't think that was too much of a lie since I truly did miss her. I had merely omitted the real reason for my reticence. I was still determined that Ruthanne was going to be the first person to hear my news. And that worried me too. Was I making the right decision? And should I even bother her with it at all since she was thousands of miles away and couldn't do anything about it? *But she needs to know,* I told myself.

She called on Sunday as I had asked. I told her the story while she patiently waited. "I've been scared because I don't know what's ahead.

I haven't told anyone yet because I wanted you to be the first to know."

"I'm so sorry you have to deal with this without me. I can't leave now."

"I know," I said. "I'll get through it. I have an appointment soon to talk with the surgeon. I'll let you know what I find out. But you can understand why I didn't tell Ortha. She'd have been on the phone as soon as I went to bed. She'd have told a hundred people right away, and I wasn't ready to deal with that yet."

"Oh, yeah. I understand."

In typical Ruthanne fashion, she had lots of advice for how to get through the next few weeks. If she couldn't be there to take charge of things, she could provide tons of ideas, and I did feel some comfort about that. She always could put things into perspective. "Follow doctor's orders, and don't overdo it. Take it easy."

As it turned out, it was a simple fix. My cancer was Stage One, which the doctor on the phone had neglected to tell me. The one piece of information that might have eased my angst, she didn't share with me. Ultimately, I had surgery followed by five weeks of radiation. That was it, except for a little more fatigue at the end of it all; ironically, ending the way it started. Even then, my fatigue was more like a day trip compared to Ruthanne's constant MS fatigue that never left her alone.

It might have saved a lot of anxiety had the examining physician mentioned the words "Stage One," either to me on the phone or to the surgeon, or both. They might have prevented the steep decline in my mental state. After the initial consultation I got on the web and looked up cancer staging and discovered that Stage One meant the cancer was contained—it had not spread to any other parts of the body. It was the surgeon's nurse who told me what stage it was. The surgeon didn't know until after he began talking about radical and invasive incisions. "We'll start at the pubis and go up to the navel. If need be, we will go around the navel and on up the midsection."

Shocked beyond disbelief, I asked, "All that for Stage One?"

"You know that?" he asked as he scrambled through the report, somewhat embarrassed.

"Your nurse told me just a bit ago."

"I'm so sorry I missed that," he said as he finally found it on the last page of the report. I should think that would have been stated on page one.

For the rest of her life, Ruthanne apologized for not having been there for my ordeal. "It's no big deal," I always reassured her. Still, she berated herself many times for not being able to help me out during my one brush with a serious medical problem.

And it wasn't a big deal. It was caught early, and I returned to a normal life almost immediately, unlike her own cancer odyssey that began a mere two years later. That diagnosis, and the next one three years after that, became big fat deals. The next fourteen years were a maze of doctors, myriad medical appointments, and procedures that would eventually take us through nine surgeries, even more chemo regimens, numerous and egregious side effects, years of chronic lymphedema, the loss of her kidneys, followed by two years of dialysis, all of which led to weekly paracentesis (draining of built-up body fluid) and weekly blood transfusions. She endured so much for so long, it amazed me and everyone who knew her how she did it. "It is what it is," she would say, or "This is the new reality."

Many times, I heard her say, "Whatever it is, we will deal with it."

She repeated that sentence often, whether it was while waiting for the results of a new PET scan, or after a car accident, or a leak in the roof. And we always dealt with it. She never saw the point in getting all worked up over things we had no control over. Her attitude helped me stay on an even keel as well. Her calmness, her matter-of-fact approach comforted me, but also astounded me.

The only time I heard her complain was in the last two years of her life when things got complicated. She went through all of it with as much grace as one can under such constant medical need. My brief journey was easy in comparison. Her extenuated journey was much more difficult, much more exacting, much more grueling, much more time consuming, and debilitating. All of this would eventually take her away from me. Who had the rougher time of it? She did, by far. So, why is it that I'm the one who's still hurting?

TRUST ME

Kate is absolutely awed by the flowers you sent. It's an enormous bouquet. You should see it. I'll take a picture of it for you.

LETTER FROM RUTHANNE TO PAT

In 1998, Ruthanne was selected to teach a group of Iowa community college students for a study abroad program in Cambridge, England for the fall semester. She and the students were assigned home stays, and Ruthanne found herself settled in with Kate. They got along quite well and began to spend some free time together.

I ordered the flowers right after I dropped her off at the airport, wanting them to be there when she arrived. What I didn't know is that while my $30 investment would have bought a modest flower arrangement here at home, it bought something enormous there.

Eventually, Ruthanne was introduced to Kate's daughter Jacque and her husband, then to Angela and Graham, and finally to Janet. Those friendships lasted long after that semester was over and we ended up traveling with four of them at different times, mostly in the United States and in Canada.

Two weeks of that semester were spent in London where Ruthanne met Gemma, her support person for all things academic. One evening, Ruthanne, Gemma and two female students went out to dinner. They parked Gemma's mini-Cooper at the curb, had dinner, and came back to find the car sandwiched between two other cars, with about six inches of free space at either end.

"Well, this is grand," said Gemma.

Ruthanne piped up, "Not to worry. You two get in front of the car, we will get in the back of it. On the count of three we will pick it up and move it sideways."

All three women looked at her like she'd sprouted pumpkins from her ears.

"There is no way we can move that car," Julie groaned.

"We'll have to wait until one of these other cars moves," the other student said.

"I agree," said Gemma. "It's wedged in there pretty tight."

"Trust me, it will work." It was a phrase I heard Ruthanne say many times in our years together. And usually, things worked out.

"Come on, trust me," begged Ruthanne. "It's just one little car against the four of us. It can't weigh much more than a thousand pounds, right? We're tough broads."

Somewhat skeptically, they took their places. It worked. They hitched that car right out of there like it was a mere basket of apples, hopped in and went on their way, quite pleased with their prowess.

I assume they learned a valuable lesson in what it meant to hang out with Ruthanne. When she said, "Trust me," she usually came through. I had my doubts throughout our years together, and it always caught me up short.

One summer Ruthanne and I were trekking around Wales and Scotland and hiked up a small mountain in Wales. We parked at the bottom, not realizing we could have taken the car up a road to the halfway point. By the time we got to the top it had begun to snow.

"It doesn't look like much yet," she said, "but I suppose we shouldn't stay too long up here."

"No," I said. "We might as well get back. I don't want to get stuck up here with two feet of snow wearing only shorts and a t-shirt."

"Well, we did bring our jackets," Ruthanne reminded me.

"But no long pants," I returned.

We still felt warm from the hike up, therefore weren't too worried about getting chilled. The temperature dropped as we descended, and by the time we got back to the halfway point, the snow had turned into serious rain.

"Now I'm cold," I complained.

"Not to worry. Let's ask that man for a ride," Ruthanne said, nodding in his direction. He was just unlocking his car.

"We're soaking wet," I whined. "He's not going to let us in that car."

"Trust me," came those ubiquitous words. "We'll get a ride."

"Well, I'm not asking."

"Watch this," she said confidently.

"You're just going to march over there and ask a stranger for a ride?" I said—to her back, since she was already on her march.

I have no idea what she said. I was standing way back out of earshot, in awe of her audacity. After a few seconds' chat, she motioned me over. We climbed in and went on our way.

She tapped me on the knee, sporting a giant grin, leaned over, and whispered, "Did Ruthanne save the day, or what?"

She always was able to see a way out of situations and was never afraid to ask a stranger for help. There wasn't anything spectacular about the ten-minute ride back down, except our driver noticed we were shivering. He turned on the heat, apologizing for the nasty weather, as if he were responsible for it. It did prompt him to ask, "Do you know how to tell it's summer in Wales?"

"No," we both answered.

"The rain gets warmer," he chuckled.

I'm guessing that's an old joke, but it was the first time I'd heard it, and I appreciated the humor and the ride. When we got to the lower car park we got out and apologized for the wet seat.

That same trip, we drove on up to Scotland, visited Ben Nevis, and hiked part of the Great Western Way, as well as a few more hills. We had started our hike near Fort William and trekked to a small village where we could catch a train back to our starting point. Hamlet would have been a better description. There were three structures—a hotel, a pub, and one other building—all sitting on one side of a gravel road. Across the road were the railroad tracks, accompanied by a platform. No building, no agent, just a platform. We saw not a soul in the hamlet, but about a dozen other people waited at the platform.

"This must be an important train stop," I said.

"It's a lot livelier than the town."

After waiting a few minutes, I walked out on the track to see if there might possibly be a train coming. You'd have thought I was trying to steal the moon. About every person waiting was yelling.

"You'll get run over."

"That train is going to be coming pretty fast."

"I wouldn't stand there if I were you."

It was only then that we noticed everyone there except us had a camera hanging on a strap around their neck. And it looked as if some of them had come halfway around the world to be there.

"What's going on?" Ruthanne asked.

"It's a special train, here all the way from China, touring the country. It's going to be here and gone in just a few seconds," said one guy.

"It should be here any second now and it will be moving very fast," said another.

We didn't know what the ruckus was all about, but we waited, and we stayed off the track, lest we give one of them a heart attack. True to their word, the train came barreling around the bend, whizzed past us, and was gone in a matter of seconds. Cameras clicked until the train could no longer be seen. Then they all left.

"Well," I said. That seems like a long way to come for twenty seconds of excitement."

"I guess," Ruthanne said. "It didn't look all that special to me."

We waited and eventually caught our own train, moving at a much more human speed. It stopped just long enough for us to board and off it went.

Once we got off the train, we drove up to the highlands, got a youth hostel room, and were hanging around outside when Ruthanne suggested we take a short walk up a hill—at 9:30 in the evening.

"It's too late to be heading out for a hike," I said. "It's almost bedtime, anyway."

"Trust me," she said. "We'll be back before it gets too dark. We'll only go up to that first crest and come back."

She was right, of course. We were so far north that it wasn't all that dark at 10:00 p.m.

A few days later, we went to a wilderness area and parked the car in a gravel lot. Ours was the only car there, which should have been an omen. We grabbed our day packs and set out. We saw some waterfalls, crossed a creek or two, found an idyllic spot to eat our packed lunch, and continued our hike. When we got to the edge of the wilderness, some three hours later, we came out onto a gravel road, with no car park and no car. "Oops," said Ruthanne. "We must have come out on the wrong path. It was supposed to be a loop."

I asked, "Well now what are we going to do, walk all the way back through and hope we come out in the right spot this time?"

"No need for that," she said. "Ruthanne will take care of it."

"How do you think you're going to do that?"

"We'll hitch a ride," she said, as if we were standing on the edge of some freeway in San Francisco and had a plethora of vehicles to choose from.

I walked to the middle of the road and with great fanfare, turned my head slowly to the left, then to the right. "Do you see one vehicle on this road? We could be here for hours waiting for a car to come along. It's mighty dismal out here. I'll bet this road only sees one car a day."

"Trust me. This looks like a well-traveled road. We'll hitch a ride in no time."

I wasn't smiling and didn't intend to until I was back in a comfortable bed somewhere. But one good glance at the road did tell me that it was well-maintained, therefore fairly well-traveled.

Within thirty seconds, a car came along. I sucked in air I was so shocked. This time I let her do her thing, still sure there wouldn't be a second car that day.

"Watch this," she said and, stuck her thumb out.

The driver, a guy about 60, slowed the car and rolled the window down, and Ruthanne explained our situation. He nodded, thought a few seconds, and said, "I think I know where your car is. Hop in. We'll take you there."

That's when we noticed another man in the car. "I'm John, and this is my father. I'm taking him to a doctor's appointment."

Ruthanne introduced us, then tapped me on the arm and said quietly, "Ruthanne always provides, right?"

I rolled my eyes. Ruthanne and John struck up a conversation, covering the usual topics new acquaintances march through when they know their time together is short. The father and I both remained silent for the five or six minutes it took to find our car. John asked where we were from.

"Des Moines, Iowa. Right in the middle of the United States," Ruthanne answered.

"What are you doing walking around out here in the middle of nowhere?" he asked.

"Hiking," Ruthanne answered. "We love to hike."

Finally, the old man spoke in what I could swear was a southern Alabama drawl but with a Scottish accent.

"It seems, like a long way, to come, for a walk."

LESSONS FROM CHILDREN

I'd like to take the whole family to Mexico. Would
spring break work for you two?

LETTER FROM ORTHA TO RUTHANNE

The most aggravating thing to me in Mexico was not being
able to read the street signs, billboards, and menus. I took only two
semesters of Spanish way back in 1987 and to this day I probably only
remember how to ask for the bathroom or the telephone…and one of
those is a moot point these days anyway.

Enchilada was a word I could read and know what it meant—
mostly. Thus, I ate more enchiladas that week than I normally eat
in a year, because I assumed no translation was necessary. Still,
I didn't always get what I thought I ordered. The food was always
good—exceptionally good—but not standardized by any means, and
certainly not your typical Taco John's. An enchilada dinner in Mexico
apparently has many interpretations.

We spent a whole week there when Ruthanne's nieces and nephews
were young, making quite an entourage. Ruthanne's mother, Ortha,
sponsored the trip by paying for airfare, hotels, and food. In addition
to the three of us, there were three more adults and five kids. We

toured the cities—the rich parts of town, the poor parts of town, and a whole lot in between. We ate foods familiar to us, since enchiladas and tacos were on every menu. We saw menu items not so familiar to us—like prickly pear and deep-fried crickets. I let those items stay right on the menu. They weren't touching my plate or palate.

One day, we all decided to go swimming at a resort with a human-made lake. It was fine and the water nice, but I was disappointed we weren't actually at a natural body of water. It was more like a resort swimming pool than a lake. Nice, but I prefer something nature has to offer. But on a vacation in a foreign country, with different cultural norms, I like to practice flexibility.

We laid out our towels and swam, sat in the sun, and relaxed. Parents helped their kids. Ortha and I mostly hung out on the beach. Ruthanne swam and played with the kids in the water. While we were there, we heard from some people lounging on the beach near us that there were some cenotes not too far away. A cenote is a natural sinkhole where a cave ceiling has collapsed.

"Can you tell us how to get there?" Norma, our sister-in-law, asked. She was the most fluent Spanish speaker.

We noted the directions and had a small family conference.

"Should we leave here now and go there for a bit?" Most adults agreed we should, so we packed up and went in search of these famous sinkholes.

Once there, we again unloaded the cars, found a spot to dump all our things, and rented snorkel gear for everyone.

It was quickly decided that the best pairing would be one adult to one kid, with one adult left over. Ruthanne's older brother had been a first-class klutz his whole life. Two years Ruthanne's senior, he would never have learned to ride a bike if not for Ruthanne teaching him. The family quickly decided he should be on his own. *Go for it. Sink or swim, buddy.*

That left five adults and five kids. The assumption was that the adult in each pair had the swimming abilities to help the kid and be able to carry out a rescue in an emergency. In my case, that assumption was far overestimated. I could swim just fine, but my confidence in rescuing a child was nil.

Four of the other adults immediately selected a kid, and I was asked if I would take Adam. At that moment, I felt like I was back in sixth grade gym class when the teacher picks two students to be captains and they take turns choosing who would be on their team. As always, someone had to be last. Adam and I, as the last to be paired, didn't actually choose each other. I was somewhat disappointed, and to this day I'm ashamed of what went through my mind at that moment.

Adam was somewhat of a problem child, prone to tantrums and other kinds of acting out. His social behavior was different than most kids I knew. I wasn't sure I could relate to him, let alone be the kind of adult the others expected me to be. I wasn't angry, but I wasn't pleased. Since then, I've learned more about Asperger's and the autism spectrum, and I've become considerably more compassionate. That day I wasn't so charitable. I resented being stuck with what I considered to be an ill-behaved child.

We all put our snorkel gear on and prepared to get into the water. The kids had been forewarned to stay close to their adult. My concern was that Adam would swim away from me and I wouldn't be able to restrain him or worse, catch him. My water skills, at best, were mediocre, and I had no idea what his skills were. *What if he panics and starts flailing? What if I panic and start flailing?* With some trepidation, I entered the water. Adam was right beside me.

We hadn't been in the water ten seconds when Adam reached out and took hold of my hand. If he could have seen my face, he might have registered my surprise. He stayed right by my side the whole time we were in the water, probably thirty to forty minutes. He didn't try to swim away from me. He didn't try to do his own thing. He didn't throw a fit. He didn't do anything that would be cause for reprimand. In a way I was bothered by the fact that there is no talking during snorkeling. Scuba divers have a kind of hand signal language used to communicate with fellow divers. Is there one for snorkelers? I had no idea if this kid was enjoying this experience. I couldn't ask. He couldn't say. It wasn't possible to read his body language. We simply continued to swim around in our quiet, underwater world until it was time to return to land, his hand still firmly in mine.

Once we were on solid ground, we grabbed our towels to dry off. Ortha began asking the kids in general what they thought of the experience. Four kids answered right away blurting out various sentiments about the colorful fish they had seen and how much fun they'd had. Noticing that Adam still hadn't said anything, Ruthanne addressed him directly.

"Adam, what did you think? Did you like it?"

And there it was, that moment in an adult's life when a valuable lesson creates itself out of thin air, wraps itself in humility, forms itself into an arrow, and then takes deadly, accurate aim for the middle of your heart.

When asked the direct question, Adam—that sweet little eight-year-old boy—didn't hesitate. He announced, "This has been the best day of my life."

MUSIC TO GO

I'm still practicing my piano lessons. I'm enclosing an article from the newspaper. Apparently, there is an increase of anti-gay bias and the article mentions that the AIDS crisis is giving bigots an excuse to act out their hatred.

LETTER FROM PAT TO RUTHANNE

After we first got keys to the house, Ruthanne took me over to look at it one more time before moving in. When I walked into the house, the first thing I saw was a new piano with a big yellow bow and ribbon on it. Actually, it was the only thing in the house, with the rest of the rooms empty and waiting for us to move our stuff in. Along with the piano came a few lessons, but they didn't last long.

Ruthanne got more use out of the piano than I did. She already knew how to play. The teacher I had was used to working with third graders and I was learning to play things like "Putt, Putt, Little Boat" and "Mary Had a Little Lamb." Several free lessons were enough for me. But that wasn't the last of the music in our lives, and I am reminded of all the music Ruthanne provided for me through the years.

I miss hearing Ruthanne play the piano for me. She played Holly

Near's "We are an Angry, Gentle People" and other music of that era. It's an easy song to love and to sing along with. I particularly liked it when she played more classical tunes like "Brian's Song" and "The Great Gate of Kiev," and I often requested them. Early in our relationship, she introduced me to the symphony, which I still enjoy today. And my car radio is always set to the Iowa Public Radio station and its offerings.

Wherever we were, whether at home or traveling, Ruthanne could drum up a little music. Our friend Dan was visiting one Thanksgiving weekend. He had been a former colleague of Ruthanne's, and knowing that he played well, she asked him to give us a short recital. I was enthralled with the music filling our living room as if we were in a concert hall. His skills far outpaced Ruthanne's. She had three years of piano lessons. He must have had far more, because he used to play for the Miss America pageant, and his skills were evident. He played bits and pieces of one classical tune after another, then some show tunes.

After about twenty minutes of serious playing, he said, "Here's something I used to do for fun. I play one tune with my right hand and another with the left hand. See if you recognize these two tunes."

I couldn't believe what was bouncing and high stepping off one end of that piano, while something else was oozing ever so smoothly off the other end. I don't know how anyone makes both hands cooperate enough to play the same tune, so what he was doing was just short of miraculous. His right hand was playing "Boogie Woogie" while his left hand was playing "The Old Rugged Cross." It seemed he could oddly pair about any two tunes together and pull it off like he was doing nothing more than drinking a glass of water. What a joyous treat.

Ruthanne continued to find music for us. We were on a large plane one day and unfortunately found our seats to be in the middle of those rows of five seats across, with more seats across the aisle to the left and others across the aisle to the right. It was a full flight. But, as usual, Ruthanne struck up a conversation with the person to her right. She found out he was part of a huge college choir traveling for a competition. "Are all your choir members on board?" she asked.

"Yes," he said, "plus our choir director."

It wasn't long before Ruthanne said, "Excuse me, excuse me," as she made her way over a couple pairs of knees and out to the aisle to visit the restroom. Pretty soon, she came back, made her way back across all those knees, sat down, and whispered, "Get ready, you are going to hear something incredible."

The choir director stood up and got everyone's attention. He introduced himself and his choir, then mentioned where they were from and where they were going. "We've been requested to sing something for you. Of course, our choir members aren't going to be in their proper sections as they would be on a stage, but we will do our best."

And they did. Thirty or more choir members stood right where they were and gave us their best. The sound bounced around the plane like it was designed for choirs. The result was a short but sweet recital. We vigorously thanked them by clapping till our hands ached. I also heard a few shouts of "Bravo." I still don't know how Ruthanne pulled that off or who she talked to, but I thoroughly enjoyed the music.

In 2003, we'd been traveling in England and Scotland and made our way to Wales where we saw some breathtaking scenery. We spent time in Cardiff and eventually visited a town called Llangollen, though it was pronounced, as near as our ears could make out, like *clan-gloflin*.

We were staying at a youth hostel. Shortly after we found our supper at a nearby pub, we came back and found the place full to the brim with other people, which is usually the way it is in hostels. We talked to a few of them and went on to our own room. At breakfast, Ruthanne discovered this group was a smaller choir from St. Andrews, also traveling and singing. There were about a dozen of them.

She couldn't let that opportunity go by. Here was another chance for a free concert. She requested, and after some discussion and hesitation, they obliged. They may have been smaller in number, and in a much smaller space, but they were no less professional in their performance than the larger choir.

Ruthanne could order up music about anywhere. During one of her many hospital stays, our church's Caring Minister coordinator asked if there was anything she needed.

"Yes," Ruthanne answered immediately. "I'd like a few members of the choir to come and sing for me."

And they did. Six or eight of them marched right into her room, arranged themselves just right, and sang for her. Unfortunately, I missed that performance. But Ruthanne described it to me, telling me who had come and what songs they had sung, and mentioning that the nursing staff and other patients enjoyed it too.

"You should have heard it. In this small room the music was beautiful. They sounded like professionals."

She was not only pleased, she was grateful. She rarely asked for anything for herself, usually choosing to be the giver. But you'd have thought someone sent the Mormon Tabernacle Choir to sing for her. Her gratitude was larger than any cathedral, her accolades even more melodious. A beautiful idea turned into a beautiful moment for all within earshot.

If music wasn't at hand, she went looking for it. There was an announcement one Sunday at church that our pianist, Bruce Martin, would be playing with a jazz band at the Botanical Gardens downtown that afternoon. Of course, we went to hear it. During a break, he talked to us for a few minutes and asked if we were jazz fans. Without missing a beat, Ruthanne said, "No, we're Bruce Martin fans." I think he blushed a bit.

Despite all this wonderful music, there was one bit of music neither of us particularly wanted to hear, though it apparently bothered her more than it did me. We were sitting in the living room when she suddenly got upset.

"I sure wish that music would stop," she said.

"What music?" I asked, because I wasn't hearing anything at the time.

"There's music all the time. I don't know if it's a neighbor or a car driving by or what, but it's always some obnoxious rock and roll stuff. I hear it when I'm here alone. "You don't hear it?"

I was so astounded I just about fell off the couch. I'd been hearing music for months, also while I was alone in the house. But unlike her, I was hearing all genres of music. I heard operas, classical, jazz, hymns, as well as rock and roll. Sometimes it was so faint I wasn't sure if I was really hearing it at all and had to sit very quietly to pick up the sounds. Other times it was clear and loud. But like her, I had no idea where it was coming from. I assumed someone nearby had an eclectic taste in music and liked it loud most of the time; or at least loud enough that we could hear it with doors and windows all shut. Until that day, I had determined to never mention it to her for fear she'd think I was slipping off the deep end of reality.

"You hear that?" I practically shouted.

"Yeah, you do too?"

I said I did but also admitted I didn't know where it was coming from. We didn't solve anything that day, but I was immensely relieved that someone else was hearing it too, and that I was still residing on this side of sanity.

I often heard voices as well—at least, one voice. There was no conversation. It was one guy talking in the manner of a radio reporter at a baseball game: enthusiastic, with that cadence that announcers develop, and somewhat louder than normal talking.

Five years after Ruthanne died, I saw a small article in the newspaper about this phenomenon. It's called pareidolia (pare-ih-DOH-lee-uh). I was startled that it had a name, and I shouted out loud, "Ruthanne, you should read...!"

Apparently, the condition is quite common. It occurs when anything makes regular sound patterns and the ear interprets those sounds as music. Ours was coming from the HVAC system. I was as dumbstruck as if someone had hit me over the head with a saxophone. Which, come to think of it, might have brought real music to my ears.

I don't hear the phantom music anymore, but I did mention to our pianist, Bruce, recently that I still enjoy his piano playing abilities. I also still enjoy an eclectic mix of music on the CD player in my car on long drives. I don't have Ruthanne around to provide music for me anymore, but I do just fine with my mix of favorites, and I still attend the symphony when I can. It beats waiting around for the HVAC system to provide me with musical entertainment.

DID YOU DO THIS?

Would you two like to go to Aruba for your 40th birthday?

LETTER FROM ORTHA TO RUTHANNE

Since it would only be the three of us celebrating this birthday, and even then, with a slice of cake, without candles, after some restaurant meal, I wanted to do something more for Ruthanne. It was her fortieth, after all, and it needed to be recognized. A card shower seemed just the right thing to do.

It sounds easy, but it wasn't. Ruthanne didn't keep an address book. She simply remembered everyone's address. Even if a friend had moved three times in the last decade, she could run through her mental list and get the current one.

But where could I find addresses for all these people? I couldn't just ask her for them. Fortunately, she corresponded with people all over the place and had boxes of letters in the closet of my sewing room.

Ruthanne possessed many skills, but the power of observation wasn't one of them. She was smart as a whip, but failed occasionally to see what was taking place in her presence. Our computer at that time was in the basement of our split-level home. The sewing room was on the top floor.

She was working on the computer, and I was supposedly making a skirt for myself. What I was really doing was going through all that correspondence, looking for the addresses of all her friends. All was going fine, when I heard her come up the stairs. The first set was carpeted, so I didn't hear her right away. Her footsteps on the second set alerted me too late to close up the box of old letters and put it back into the closet. I rushed over to my sewing machine as if nothing else in the world was going on, leaving the open box sitting on a chair.

She came in and asked how my project was going. Had she been more observant, she'd have noticed I hadn't made much progress on a simple A-line skirt. It consisted of two pieces of fabric sewed together with a waistband and a hem. It should have taken no more than an hour to lay the fabric out, pin the pattern to it, cut it out, and assemble the thing.

"Fine," I said. After a few minutes hanging out chatting about nothing, she turned to leave. It was then that she noticed the box and I thought for sure I had been caught. I kept on sewing.

"Oh, I wonder when I left this here. I'll put it away later." She folded the flaps into place and left the room. I couldn't believe my luck. Anyone else would have asked why it was there and what was I doing with it. But she went back downstairs, and I eventually got my list, leaving the box right where it was. I sent letters to everyone I could think of asking them to send a card to arrive at our house sometime during the week we were to be gone. I also asked them to pass the word on to other friends I might not have known about. I asked Ortha, as well, to alert lots of family friends. I sent notes to all of Ruthanne's colleagues and many of our church friends. I must have sent out fifty or more letters, plus what I could by email.

We had a whole week to spend on an island measuring a mere six by twenty miles. We arrived in the early evening, and during the taxi ride to the timeshare apartment, I noticed the landscape. I saw that the western world had thundered onto what I had hoped would be a quaint, romantic little slice of paradise. Instead, nearly every American fast food joint imaginable populated the city of Oranjestad, Aruba. Tall buildings pierced the sky as if to announce, *You're in the big city now.* I had wanted to see thatched roofs and scantily dressed women carrying huge trays of whole fruit on their heads.

We did some snorkeling and swimming and a bit of touring. When we went to the beach, the attendant took one look at us, making note of our lily-white skin, handed us beach towels and took us directly to the shade of a nice large tree. While he said nothing about his choice, we knew he was right. A few years earlier, Ruthanne had visited a friend in Jamaica where she had sat beneath any shade tree she could find. Still, she came home with sunburned leaf prints all over her thighs and a few on her arms. We quietly accepted our assigned spots there in Aruba.

All too soon it was time to go home. My neighbor, Brenda, was collecting our mail, and I was anxious to go get it so Ruthanne could see what we'd done.

"I'm going over to Brenda's to get the mail," I said.

"It's 9:00. It can wait until morning, can't it?"

"She's probably still up," I said. "I'll go get it now."

I brought back two paper grocery sacks of mail and set them down beside Ruthanne and encouraged her to look at some of it. What happened next was unbelievable.

"Todd sent me a birthday card. I didn't know he knew my birthdate. Steph sent me a card. I haven't heard from her in a decade. Here's one from Noli. She doesn't usually send me birthday cards. I haven't heard from Lori since she moved to Nebraska. There are a lot of cards in here. I wonder how some of these people knew it was my birthday."

This went on for at least fifteen minutes while Ortha and I kept exchanging glances, wondering when Ruthanne would catch on that none of this was random or coincidence. Ortha kept shaking her head and making gestures as if to say, *I can't believe this.* Her eyes got big a couple of times, her mouth opened in surprise, she rolled her eyes a couple of times, and still Ruthanne kept reading and making comments about people she hadn't heard from in a very long time. Ortha and I were beginning to think she had sunburned her brain while in Aruba.

As smart at Ruthanne was, I wondered about her perception. I worked with a woman who had worked at the community college with Ruthanne several years before. "I was trying to hit on her," said Diane. "But she never seemed to catch on."

"Nope," I said. "You'd have to write her a note for her to catch on to that."

Finally, after what seemed an eternity, with nearly a whole sack of mail opened, Ruthanne looked over at me with a grin and said, "Did you do this?"

Hallelujah. Later, I counted well over 100 cards. Not too bad for a novice sleuth. And I still shake my head wondering why it took this incredibly smart woman so long to catch on.

PROCURING FOOD

When you get here, I'd like to take you up the Coffee Creek Trail to meet my friends Dave and Sandy. It's a cool cabin with all the boards nailed on vertically rather than horizontally.

LETTER FROM RUTHANNE TO PAT

"You know," I said, sitting in that very same wilderness one evening, "with all the hiking and backpacking we've done, I'm surprised you've never had us foraging or fishing."

"Oh, I had enough of that in Guyana the summer I was sixteen. If we wanted to eat, we had to procure it from nature. There were no grocery stores in the jungle. There was plenty of guava, but if we wanted anything else we had to grow it or kill it."

"So, what did you eat?" I asked.

"Well, I killed a baby alligator once. Barry and I were in the coreal, that's sort of like a canoe, on the Berbice river, and we saw it nearby. He asked me if I thought I could take it. Probably, I said. It's not that big, but it's the piranhas I'm more worried about."

"So, how did you do it?" I asked.

"We always kept a hunting knife in the coreal. I put it in my teeth, swashbuckler style, jumped into the river, wrestled the alligator, slit its throat, tossed it into the coreal and jumped back in as quickly as I could."

"You didn't get bitten?" I asked, startled.

"No, but by the time I got back to the coreal, the piranhas were gathering. Fresh blood draws them that fast. The whole thing probably took less than a minute. Barry helped pull me back into the coreal."

"That was nice of him. What else did you eat?"

"Once, one of the boys and I were walking down the road and saw a dead dog. It was our turn to fix supper that night. It wasn't bloated and there were no flies on it, so we knew it was a pretty fresh kill. We took it home, cleaned it, got rid of the bones, put a whole lot of curry on it and cooked it."

"What did the others think of that?"

"They knew enough not to ask, and we didn't say."

"It must have been tough surviving in that environment," I mused out loud.

"In a way, it was, but I think it also saved my life."

"How?"

"Before I went to Guyana, I was suicidal. Guyana taught me to trust my brain and my instincts. It taught me that I could get through a lot of tough situations. I learned to keep going, no matter how bleak things seem."

"Did your parents know you were suicidal?" I asked.

"I don't know. Maybe."

"I think they must have. Why else would they let a sixteen-year-old girl travel alone thousands of miles away to unknown territory to spend a summer in the jungle having to scrounge for food?"

"You could be right," she mused.

COVID—NO PROBLEM

If Ruthanne had lived to experience the Covid-19 situation, she would have taken it in stride. She spent the last fourteen years of her life being around medical people and wearing masks, gloves, gowns, and paper shoes. After all those surgeries and many rounds of chemo, radiation, x-rays, dialysis, and lymphedema treatment, she wouldn't have blinked at the orders to wear a mask, wash hands frequently, and stay away from sick people.

In the thirty years I knew her, she never touched an elevator button with her fingertips. It was always the middle knuckle of her non-dominant left hand. "You don't know how many people touch those buttons every day," she expounded often.

In any building with fewer than four floors, she often opted to take the stairs, but never used the handrails. "You don't know how many people touch those railings every day, and you don't know how often they get cleaned. Trust your legs to do the work." That last one was a carryover from her backpacking days of climbing mountains, hills, and other tough terrain.

If she went into a business sporting those large door handles that looked like a giant squared off backwards C, she always grabbed it at the very bottom, because fewer people grab the handle there. When leaving a building with panic bars on the doors, she never pushed the bar with her hands but leaned into it with the side of her body. "You don't know how many…"

At least twenty years ago we were at a large outdoor gathering with hundreds of other people for a weekend. When there was news of an outbreak of shigella, an incredibly severe intestinal malady, Ruthanne instructed me to wash my hands with soapy water and rub them for at least twenty seconds. "But this water's cold," I said.

"That doesn't matter," she responded. "It's the rubbing action with the soap that does it. And it needs to be at least twenty seconds, minimum." I followed instructions. We never got shigella.

In any hotel room, Ruthanne always kept her shoes on until bedtime. She would never have walked around barefoot in one of those rooms, no matter how nice and clean the hotel appeared to be.

In a restaurant with cloth napkins, of course they went on our laps, but in a fast food place when we left the napkin on the table, she was quite conscious of which side of it she was using to wipe her mouth. That side never touched the table.

These days in every parking lot, I see a mask or two, abandoned, purposely tossed, or accidentally dropped. No one is picking these things up. And as ardent as Ruthanne was about cleaning up our world, I'm quite certain she would never have picked them up either. "You never know who…"

None of our recommended Covid safety precautions would have bothered her in the least, but the social distancing might have given her pause. We understood and lived by the idea that everyone needs "alone" time now and then—personal time, a time of recentering the mind. But two people being sequestered in the same house for weeks or months at a time might have caused serious harm to her psyche. She was a social person and loved being around people. Isolation might have killed her, had the cancer not beaten her to it.

CLUTTER

I'm sorry my stuff takes up most of the space in this house. You aren't going to kick me out because of all my clutter, are you?

CARD FROM RUTHANNE TO PAT

I recently read a short note on Facebook that said a cluttered desk is a sign of high intelligence. It named a few people, including Einstein, who on the day of his death had an extremely cluttered desk. Apparently, science has found a link between clutter and extremely high IQ. I truly believe that, because Ruthanne had both high intelligence and a messy desk. Every flat surface became her filing system, both at home and at work. Her explanation was that were she to organize and file all those papers, she would want to do it right, and there was never enough time to do it right, so she left it as it was.

When I am expecting company, I scoop up piles of papers and stuff them into any drawer that will accommodate them. The cool thing is that when I decide to go through that pile of papers, about eighty percent of it can go right to the recycling bin. No filing required. It saves me lots of time.

Ruthanne's students were in awe of her filing system. She'd have a stack of papers a foot tall, but when asked for last week's class handout, she knew within a few sheets of paper just where to pull from the stack. I was in awe of that.

When I was living in Peoria and we were trading visits, I remember a weekend when I had spent quite some time getting my apartment tidied up. She came in with several bags of papers, plus her overnight bag. She sat in the middle of the living room floor, and I did the same. Those were the days when we could get down on the floor with full confidence of being able to get back up again.

At that point, she was working on her Ed.S. degree. She started taking papers out of all those bags, showing them to me, explaining what they were, and placing them on the floor until she had almost made a complete circle around herself. It was like she had made her own paper halo, though around her crossed legs rather than her head. That was in the early years of our relationship, and I can still see her either in a chair or on the floor with her stuff around her. I wonder if there is some psychological meaning in that, somewhat like a comfort blanket or a favorite toy. It wouldn't surprise me.

I answered her original comment, jokingly, "Well you can stay, but some you your stuff might need to go."

I'd still take her back though, papers and all. The clutter, the long stories, and yes, all the environmental issues I could live with again. I still do most of the environmental stuff, except with the use of two paper towels, not one. Despite the insistence that I did way too much on her behalf, I never saw any of it as a chore. I'd do it all again, given the chance. Things were easier when there were two of us coping with the world no matter how much clutter there was.

APOLOGIES

I value you in so many ways and I'm sorry when I'm not cheerful, or friendly—and at how often I lose things and panic or rage because of my absentmindedness. Maybe I'll adjust and accept it one of these days.

LETTER FROM RUTHANNE TO PAT

She never did. Her MS disturbed her every day, because it altered, affected, and disturbed what she considered her most valuable asset: her brain. Her superb intellectual abilities allowed her to talk to people of all professions, people she encountered in everyday activities and all sorts of medical people. They were always impressed with her command of medical terminology. They would ask her medical history and she managed to rattle off important dates, diagnoses, and eventual results. I can't do that. With all these mental abilities, she still saw MS as her biggest foe.

From her initial apology in that letter, she reverts to sentiments again. *And thank you for sharing your kids and their significant creatures with me. I often feel as if I have a family and that's neat. Thanks for all your help in C.R. with mom over the years, and with her apartment, the record keeping and the PC/spreadsheet chaos.*

In typical Ruthanne fashion, she ends with several sentiments that go straight to the heart. *I will love you the rest of my life.*

I loved Ruthanne's way with words and her total appreciation for all the virtues she saw in me. Sometimes I think she put me on a pedestal that wasn't always easy to live up to. In a previous letter, dated September 1989, she says, *I just want to take a little time to remind you how important you are to me. I don't mean the little (and not so little) things—laundry, dishes, groceries, phone calls, cleaning up the apartment, etc. I mean even more your concern, love, and steady support. Your interest in my life and work, your caring for me in all my moods, your cuteness and tender smiles, your reassuring hugs and touches, your willingness—even, sometimes eagerness to help with planning, coordinating, and grading. I appreciate all that and more. And I consider myself one of the luckiest, most blessed people in the world to have you for a life partner.*

In a later letter she continued the praise for me, but also cast doubts about her own sense of worth. *Sometimes you seem so self-sufficient I'm amazed you want/need/like me around.*

All that was in reference to the MS. She went on to list several other of my attributes in dealing with the world in general. Her sentiments and how easily she handed them out reminded me of the kind of person she was.

Throughout our thirty years together, she was consistently generous with compliments. It wasn't just talk. She truly meant them, and she was always grateful I was there to help her manage life's issues. She also thought, erroneously, that I put more energy and work into our relationship than she did. My argument always was, "We each do what we know."

Ruthanne truly was my biggest advocate. I mentioned this one day to my friend Carol, who immediately responded, "And she was very good at it."

In all those years I didn't know she was singing my praises to other people, or that they would remember it.

Ruthanne generally thought I could just about walk on water. (I knew I did not.) She was always the more romantic one, and her letters demonstrate that. Perhaps that's the result of her upbringing. She grew up in a family where the parents truly loved each other and demonstrated it every day for their children. I never saw that kind of affection growing up. What I saw was the power of one person over everyone else in the house. Did this cause problems in our relationship over the years? It did. She asked once, "Do you even love me anymore?"

"I love you as much as I can love anyone."

She yearned for affection. I yearned for validation. I hope we both got what we needed. If I've learned anything over the years, it's that we are all flawed in some way. I recently made a comment to my friend Linda that we all seem to assume other people lead charmed lives, when in fact, we all have our problems. If we're lucky, we figure it out.

Then once again, in the next letter I pull out of the box, Ruthanne plants herself smack in the middle of my heart with the last sentence of the letter. *Save this and pull it out anytime you feel low or lonely or uncared for. I value you. Don't forget that.*

How do I end this story? I'm not sure, except to say that right now on this day I do feel low and lonely and uncared for. I know it's only temporary. I know it will go away and tomorrow might be a more cheerful day. I do miss the sentiments from all those letters and cards. I miss the complete abandon with which she loved me. I miss all the cheer she brought into my life. I miss the complete trust she had in me. I miss all the beautiful nicknames she gave me, her favorite being Bootter. I miss all of it.

Being a sucker for punishment—or is it sentiment? Or maybe more validation?—I pulled out one more letter where she says, *I admire everything about you.*

She goes on to say, *I admire the way you handle your professional duties, and your amazing public speaking abilities, plus your organizational skills and leadership skills.*

As if she hadn't already sung my praises enough, she adds another bit of admiration. *So, remember how much I love you. And remember that I love even more things about you than this letter says.*

These are all tender reminders of the kind of person Ruthanne was. But it was the last sentence of this particular letter that splintered my heart and made me stop reading. I couldn't see through the tears or endure the immediate thundering emotions it evoked. The lump in my throat nearly suffocated me. My heart both swelled and contracted at the same time, like it didn't know how to react. I fell back against the wall and let all that grief pour out, still holding that letter in my hand like I thought it might bring her back. She had written, *Even on the darkest days, even if I'm dead and you're alive, let my love help sustain you.*

ACKNOWLEDGMENTS

I'd like to thank all my friends and family for hanging in there with me for the last several years while I talked of finishing this book.

Thanks go out to Anne Fleck, my developmental editor, who also organized the Write to Publish writing group, giving us many lessons on how to become better writers.

The Okoboji Writer's Retreat (OWR) has helped me understand many aspects of the writing process. It's where I learned I wasn't writing a true memoir with the narrative arc, but that my vignettes were indeed a valuable way to tell a story. OWR is also where I learned there was such a thing as a writing coach.

Thus, I met Jackie Haley who helped me put my manuscript into a cohesive order.

Last but not least I want to give a big thank you to my editor, Leigh Michaels who taught me get how to get rid of redundancies, go easy on the metaphors, and clean up a few bad writing habits.

ABOUT THE AUTHOR

As a camp director for Moingona Girl Scouts, Patricia L. Headley was supervising college students, while she had only a high school diploma. This lead her to start thinking about pursuing an education. At the same time, her marriage was ending. With two daughters in high school, she knew she had to get a job or return to school. She chose school. During her second year of college, Pat met Ruthanne and realized her years-long suspicions were true. The two women became friends and eventually partners. Pat knew her life was about to change. Ruthanne encouraged Pat to think beyond the AA degree, and she went on to earn a Bachelor's Degree in Leisure Studies from The University of Iowa, and a Master's Degree in Higher Education from Drake University. Before Pat retired she was a grant writer for Meskwaki Nation—Sac & Fox Tribe of the Mississippi in Iowa. Now Pat focuses on sharing stories from her life.

Printed in the USA
CPSIA information can be obtained
at www.ICGtesting.com
LVHW051453040624
782221LV00019B/309